Biscuit Joiner Handbook

REVISED EDITION

Hugh Foster

Sterling Publishing Co., Inc.   New York

Dedicated, with affection,
to my bride of 27 years.

Library of Congress Cataloging-in-Publication Data

Foster, Hugh.
   Biscuit joiner handbook / Hugh Foster. — Rev. ed.
     p. cm.
   Includes index.
   ISBN 0-8069-0450-X
   1. Woodworking tools. 2. Joinery. I. Title.
TT186.F67 1993b
684′.083—dc20
                                                          93–41250
                                                             CIP

Edited by Michael Cea

10 9 8 7 6 5 4 3 2

Published by Sterling Publishing Company, Inc.
387 Park Avenue South, New York, N.Y. 10016
© 1995 by Hugh Foster
Distributed in Canada by Sterling Publishing
% Canadian Manda Group, One Atlantic Avenue, Suite 105
Toronto, Ontario, Canada M6K 3E7
Distributed in Great Britain and Europe by Cassell PLC
Wellington House, 125 Strand, London WC2R 0BB, England
Distributed in Australia by Capricorn Link (Australia) Pty Ltd.
P.O. Box 6651, Baulkham Hills, Business Centre, NSW 2153, Australia

Sterling ISBN 0-8069-0450-X

Contents

Metric Conversion

Inches to Millimetres and Centimetres

MM—millimetres   *CM—centimetres*

Inches	MM	CM	Inches	CM	Inches	CM
1/8	3	0.3	9	22.9	30	76.2
1/4	6	0.6	10	25.4	31	78.7
3/8	10	1.0	11	27.9	32	81.3
1/2	13	1.3	12	30.5	33	83.8
5/8	16	1.6	13	33.0	34	86.4
3/4	19	1.9	14	35.6	35	88.9
7/8	22	2.2	15	38.1	36	91.4
1	25	2.5	16	40.6	37	94.0
1¼	32	3.2	17	43.2	38	96.5
1½	38	3.8	18	45.7	39	99.1
1¾	44	4.4	19	48.3	40	101.6
2	51	5.1	20	50.8	41	104.1
2½	64	6.4	21	53.3	42	106.7
3	76	7.6	22	55.9	43	109.2
3½	89	8.9	23	58.4	44	111.8
4	102	10.2	24	61.0	45	114.3
4½	114	11.4	25	63.5	46	116.8
5	127	12.7	26	66.0	47	119.4
6	152	15.2	27	68.6	48	121.9
7	178	17.8	28	71.1	49	124.5
8	203	20.3	29	73.7	50	127.0

Introduction

When the joiner first arrived on the United States market in the mid-1970s, it was easy to understand why many considered it just another expensive and extravagant gadget. Since then it has been refined, and its price, relative to the cost of labor, has become far more reasonable. It is now available to and can be afforded by the home craftsman, with the result that the tool has become almost as essential to the serious woodworker as a cordless electric drill.

A plate joiner is not really used in the same way as other tools in the workshop (Illus. 1-1). A well-known woodworker whom I know has had a joiner for years. He says that he'll often go most of the year without using it, but will then use a couple of boxes of biscuits within a week. Biscuits are the thin, elliptical wooden wafers that are used to join the slots cut by the joiner. I use my joiners a great

Illus. 1-1. A biscuit joiner can be used to quickly make sturdy, accurate joints.

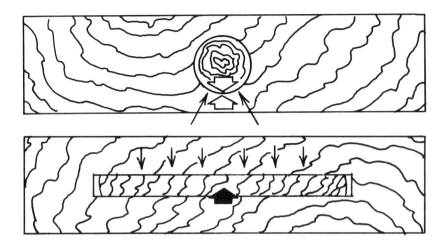

Illus. 1-2. This drawing compares the load-bearing capability of a dowel joint (top) to that of a biscuit joint (bottom).

deal more, because I like the strength and accurate alignment that joining provides. Whether you use your joiner often or only occasionally, you'll find that it is a very productive tool, primarily because it saves time.

Biscuits are approximately twice the price of commercial dowel pegs and markedly more expensive than shop-prepared dowel pegs. However, in today's workshop, material costs are just a small fraction of the project's total cost. Woodworkers have to work quickly, neatly, and efficiently, all of which is accomplished with the joiner. It saves time, which translates to a savings in money. For example, I can cut dovetails by hand at a rate of about a foot and a half an hour (both pieces), and my cuts fit fairly well, so I waste little time during assembly. However, I can make a perpendicular biscuited joint that fits perfectly well in under a minute per foot and a half. And this biscuited joint is extremely strong (Illus. 1-2 and 1-3).

Illus. 1-3. This broken joint indicates how strong biscuit joints are. Under great stress, the wood broke before the joint did.

Illus. 1-4. This biscuit-joined compact disc organizer took less than 15 minutes to cut out and assemble. If other joinery were used, this project would have been much more difficult to make. Note that it is hard to detect how the eight pieces are connected. Also note that the pieces should have been sanded before assembly.

If you're a woodworking student or teacher, you probably know that one of the perennial problems in a school shop is the amount of time wasted while students await their turns to accomplish each woodworking task. One way to expedite this process is to put four to six inexpensive plate joiners in the woodworking classroom and teach students to use them rather than rely on older, more time-consuming methods. The joiner may well double the project output of the class and make the students more interested in woodworking—not to mention more employable and efficient woodworkers.

The joiner also has other advantages. Before I bought one, there were certain kinds of joints that I avoided making. For example, I very seldom used mitre joints in a carcass application. Compound mitres were even harder to hold together, no matter how attractive they might have been. With the joiner, it is now easy to make these joints.

Virtually all assemblies go together more easily when fastened with the joiner rather than by the more conventional methods. It will probably also make the project more affordable for your customer. Illus. 1-4 shows a compact disc organizer that was assembled with no fasteners other than joining biscuits. Just a few years ago, this piece would have been far more difficult to make, much less produce in quantity.

Illus. 1-5. A dust collection kit should be used on your joiner, which will otherwise deposit dust all over your work area.

Of equal importance with speed and productivity is the issue of safety. After hundreds of hours of experimenting with plate joiners, I am convinced that they are among the safest tools in the shop, safer than any of the other portable tools, including the belt sander. However, like routers, belt sanders, and most other electrically powered tools, plate joiners are loud. Most of them run around 95 dB (decibels). To put this figure in relative terms, remember that 100 dB is the noise level for a very noisy factory, 65 dB that of normal conversation in a busy office, and 35 dB that of a quiet room. Operators should wear some type of hearing protection.

Plate joining generates a lot of dust in shops (Illus. 1-5). Some of the manufacturers discussed in the second section offer a fairly expensive dust-collection attachment. If you are a left-handed operator, this option is really more of a necessity. It's not always necessary to buy the joiner manufacturer's dust-collection kit; Bosch has for years marketed the Air-Sweep® dust hose, which comes with a malleable fitting that can be rather readily adapted to nearly all the portable joiners.

There are many advantages to a chip-extraction or dust-collection system. The handiest way to use it is to attach it to the joiner's power cord with either tie-downs or duct tape, and then put the extension cord that you're using to run the joiner near the intake on the vacuum.

In the first part of this book, the basics of joiner use are explored. This includes the history of joiners, how they work, how to use them, and a discussion of biscuits, which are, fortunately, completely interchangeable from brand to brand. In the second section, I examine all the commercially available joiners and their accessories, and discuss how to comparison-shop for a joiner. The final section deals with cutting techniques and covers the following: safety and maintenance procedures; procedures for making various kinds of joints, including butt and mitre joints; ways to adapt your machine to various nonstandard applications; and project on which to try your skills.

In the following pages the terms plate joiner and biscuit joiner should be understood to refer simply to a joiner. The thin, elliptical wooden wafers (also called plates or splines) used for joining the slots cut by the joiner will be called biscuits.

Safety Techniques

Woodworking is a potentially dangerous activity. Cutters are sharp, and high-power motors can move them at very fast speeds. Shop accidents may have a number of different causes which include (but are not limited to) operator error (which includes carelessness and haste) and equipment failure.

Woodworking machines are designed with safety in mind. If you use your tools in the way they were intended, you minimize the possibility of being hurt by them. I believe the biscuit joiner is one of the safest tools in the shop, but if you keep these following points in mind, you will ensure a safer working environment:

1. Before using your joiner, read and understand its operations manual. A good manual will describe techniques and procedures that will help to keep you safe.
2. Keep your cutters sharp and maintain them properly. Dull tools force you to exert extra pressure when you cut. This makes you

more likely to slip and, thereby, get your hands in the way of the cutting edge.

3. Clamp your work to a bench so you can use both hands to guide the tool. I have seen many woodworkers holding a piece in one hand while operating a joiner on it with the other. Particularly with small pieces, *this is very dangerous!*

4. Wear the proper safety equipment when woodworking. Always wear safety glasses or goggles. When using a tool that throws lots of chips, wear a face shield as well. When using a tool as loud as a joiner, wear hearing protection. Wear a dust mask whenever you're sanding or doing operations that produce lots of dust. If there is a dust collector available for a tool, use it *every time you switch on the tool.*

5. Wear steel-tipped shoes when you are woodworking. Don't wear loose clothing. Roll up your sleeves. If you have long hair, tie it back. Anything loose can be pulled into a cutter if it gets caught. Don't wear jewelry, not even a ring.

6. Use the D handle on your joiner. It is part of the joiner's safety equipment. By now, you've seen many photos of the joiner being held by the motor housing for a one-handed operation. To ensure your complete safety, hold the tool by the motor housing *and* by the D handle. If this accomplishes nothing else, it ensures that you won't be holding a piece so small that the biscuit joiner's blade will go through it when you make the plunge cut.

7. Do not do any woodworking if you have taken drugs or alcohol. Even over-the-counter and prescription drugs can cause drowsiness and other effects that would make it dangerous to use woodworking tools, so read the labels and follow your doctor's advice.

8. Most important, pay attention to what you're doing. Let your good sense be your guide. Think through each procedure before you do it. If you feel it presents a safety hazard, find an alternative procedure.

Remember, it's important to think about safety on a regular, ongoing basis. Only your constant vigilance will protect you from injury in the woodworking shop.

Basics

1
Historical Overview

The history of biscuit joinery can be traced back to 1956, when Herman Steiner, a Swiss cabinetmaker, started manufacturing wood-joining plates under the brand name Lamello. (The name Lamello was derived from the German word *lamelle*, which translates to "thin plate.") By 1969, the privately owned company had been transformed into Steiner Lamello Ltd., and began to manufacture a portable groove-milling machine. Four years later, the company had grown enough to move into a new plant in Bubendorf, 15 miles from Basel, Switzerland. By 1987, the company had grown to 40 employees and was building a second production plant.

From the moment it started manufacturing joiners up until today, Lamello has constantly worked to upgrade its products, which include the Lamello Top-Ten, the Lamello Standard-Ten and Cobra models, as well as a clamping system, centering awl, and other accessories.

In 1982, the Spanish firm Virutex began fabricating the O-81 joiner, a high-quality fixed-angle joiner which has consistently sold for about half the price of the Lamello Top. This tool has proved enormously popular in the United States as elsewhere.

As of this printing, many other manufacturers have started marketing biscuit joiners. These include Porter-Cable, Elu, Freud, PrinceCraft, Dewalt, Sears, Skil, Wolfcraft, and Ryobi. These are discussed in the second section.

Though its history is short, the plate joiner has undergone drastic improvement from its original entry into the marketplace. It is now considered a time-saving, efficient tool, and is used in many workshops. In the following pages, you will discover why.

2
How Joiners Work

A joiner is basically a 4-inch die-grinder-like device with a special spring-loaded faceplate that sets the depth for plunge-cutting (Illus. 2-1). Short spurs grab the workpiece while the blade plunges through the faceplate to make just the right cut for a biscuit. The biscuits work like dowels and splines to help adjoining surfaces line up flush. (See the next chapter.)

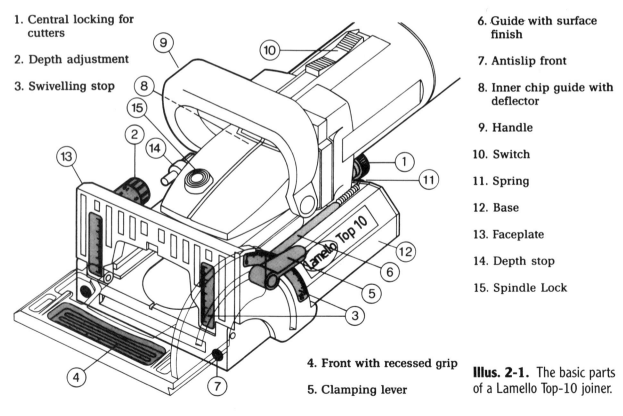

1. Central locking for cutters

2. Depth adjustment

3. Swivelling stop

4. Front with recessed grip

5. Clamping lever

6. Guide with surface finish

7. Antislip front

8. Inner chip guide with deflector

9. Handle

10. Switch

11. Spring

12. Base

13. Faceplate

14. Depth stop

15. Spindle Lock

Illus. 2-1. The basic parts of a Lamello Top-10 joiner.

The joiner provides a fast, easy, and accurate way to join wood in situations that might otherwise call for a mortise-and-tenon joint, a tongue-and-groove joint, or dowels. Though it is known for making quick, accurate butt joints, it can do much more. For example, with the joiner, edge-to-edge gluing of joints and splined mitres can be made stronger and will be easier to align.

There are basically two kinds of joiners (Illus. 2-2). The most commonly available kind—the Lamello, Virutex, Freud, and Porter-Cable models—plunges straight into its slotting cut. Another kind, for example the Bosch and Elu models, pivots into its biscuit-slotting cut. This is basically a disadvantage, though this kind of joiner is able to make grooving cuts and certain kinds of cutoffs more easily than the plunging joiner.

The spring-loaded centering pins, which are a great aid to accurate biscuit joining, help to keep all the nonpivoting joiners from moving as you make the plunge cut. These pins can be easily removed when you do other slotting work. Simply remove the faceplate by loosening two screws on the top and removing two screws from the face; the springs and pins will fall out. You can replace the faceplate for slotting to a maximum depth of $^{13}/_{16}$ inch; with the pins removed, the joiner does this much more handily than the portable circular saw.

Illus. 2-2. At left is a Makita grinder. At right is a Lamello joiner.

Illus. 2-3. The depth-of-cut scale on the Virutex 081 joiner. This scale is representative of those on the other straight-plunging joiners with the exception of the Lamello Junior.

Adjusting the Depth of Cut

Before operating the joiner, check, and if necessary, adjust its depth of cut. All the joiners that plunge straight in have the same type of depth-of-cut scale. Illus. 2-3 shows the depth-of-cut scale on the Virutex O-81.

The depth-of-cut scale is marked for number 0, number 10, and number 20 biscuits, and you can quickly adjust it by simply pulling the depth-gauge plunger towards the front of the machine and twisting it to whichever position you desire before returning it to the working position.

The depth-of-cut scale on joiners that plunge straight in can be fine-adjusted with a pair of knurled jamb nuts. Make this adjustment every time after you remove the blade cover, and check it periodically.

On the angle-in joiners, adjust the depth of cut by tightening or loosening the depth-of-cut screw to specific places on a scale. A clockwise adjustment makes the depth of cut shallower; a counter-

Illus. 2-4. The depth-of-cut scale on the Elu joiner, an angle-in joiner.

clockwise rotation makes the cut deeper. Illus. 2-4 shows the adjuster on the Elu model 3380.

With either type of joiner, it is easier to set the depth of cut with a number 20 biscuit that you have sawn in half lengthwise rather than with a ruler. After you have set the depth of cut, you are ready to cut all three sizes of biscuits. Adjust the depth of cut with the plunger, and occasionally check the fine-adjustment setting.

Making the Joint

To make a joint, mark out the pieces to be joined two inches from either end and about four inches apart between the outer two marks (Illus. 2-5). This can be done with a scale or by eye; after you have used the machine for approximately an hour you will be able to mark out quite handily by eye. The marking out does not have to be elaborate.

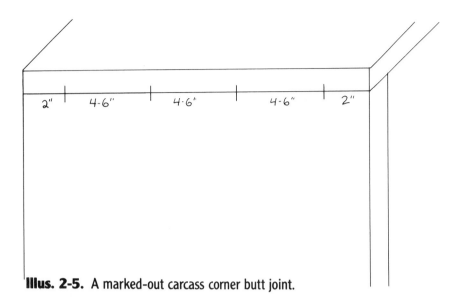

Illus. 2-5. A marked-out carcass corner butt joint.

Accurate setup is the key to accurate work. Cut out the pieces so that they will fit well when they are assembled. Take extra care when you cut them; this meticulousness will be rewarded when you begin joining them.

After you have cut out the pieces, proceed to mark out the joint. Mark to the sides of the joint rather than to its center. Simple pencil scribes made with a template, ruler, or by eye are adequate.

Lay out the joints logically. Since you are marking the sides of the joints, use the same side all the time. Mark clearly which pieces go where. Don't rely on your memory.

To cut the joints, set up the spacing of the cuts with the work and the tool both flat on the bench; this position allows you to center the cut in ¾-inch stock (the most commonly used wood thickness) and permits bilayered joining in thicker stock. If you need more than two layers, further adjustments can be made.

Though there are "square" guides on each joiner, they are not always enough to guarantee that the joint will be square, so a "stacked" setup gauge is advisable (Illus. 2-6). If the slots on the mating pieces aren't exactly parallel, the pieces will not join accurately or at all. In some cases, it is more than the middle that is out of alignment. For example, a ³⁄₃₂-inch miscut turns out to be a ³⁄₁₆-inch error when the pieces are joined, so the joint obviously won't work.

Illus. 2-6. It's a good idea to make a set of setup blocks such as the one shown here on the bottom. They only have to be 6–8 inches long, 2–4 inches wide, and the thickness of the stock that's most commonly worked.

Illus. 2-7. This is all the glue that most biscuited joints require.

Whichever way you cut the joints, they glue up alike. Glue carefully. Gluing inside the biscuit slot, as shown in Illus. 2-7, is usually sufficient except when you are using biscuit joinery to align the board for edge-gluing.

Illus. 2-8 shows a box with a divider. Let's discus the procedures for gluing it. Lay one of the pieces that will carry the insert on its side. Glue only the slots; run a fair bead of glue down each side of the slot or use a special biscuit-joining glue bottle. (See pages

Illus. 2-8. A Lamello glue bottle was used to glue together this small carcass unit. The total joining time was less than five minutes. The Lamello glue bottle is discussed in Chapter 25.

188–191). Insert the biscuits in each slot and then glue the biscuits on the pieces to be attached. Attach them immediately. Apply the next batch of glue and biscuits, and finish the assembly. It takes longer to describe the process than it does to do it.

It is a good idea to test-fit the piece with dry biscuits before gluing. To accommodate the glue, cut the grooves a bit deeper than half the biscuit's width; this also makes them slightly longer than the biscuit, thus allowing nearly a quarter inch of lengthwise play so that you can adjust the pieces to be flush at the ends.

A joint fastened with biscuits is extremely hard to realign. After it has been glued and clamped for just ten minutes in warm weather with a fast-set glue, realignment might be impossible. Chiselling firmly planted biscuits is extremely difficult, even with a razor-sharp chisel, so plan carefully.

3
The Joining Biscuit

While there are additional sizes of biscuits available today, it's still safe to say that for general woodworking biscuits come in three basic sizes. A number 0 biscuit is ⅝ inch wide × 1¾ inches long. A number 10 biscuit is ¾ inch wide × 2⅛ inches long. A number 20 biscuit is ¹⁵⁄₁₆ inch wide × 2⅜ inches long. The other sizes, much less commonly available, are discussed later in this chapter.

As measured with a surface gauge, each biscuit is .148 inch thick, and, though thinner than the ⁵⁄₃₂-inch saw blade that cuts the slots, it swells rapidly when in contact with moisture to .164 inch, enough to grip the slots tenaciously.

When the biscuit is inside the slot, the result is a joint that's very sound mechanically, which is essential. In fact, a biscuited joint after just 20 minutes of clamping is stronger than a dowelled or splined joint and as strong as standard mortise-and-tenon joints, which are harder to make.

Though some companies insist that their brands of biscuits be used with their joiners, any brand of biscuit will work with any brand of joiner. Illus. 3-1 compares generic, Porter-Cable, and Lamello biscuits, and a Lamello clamping biscuit, which is shown for size comparison.

When first starting out, most woodworkers would do well to buy a package of mixed biscuits, which generally includes 250 each of numbers 0 and 10 and 500 of number 20. Most of us will use all the number 20 biscuits long before using the smaller sizes, and then purchase a box containing 1,000 number 20 biscuits. It's a good idea to keep a spare package of the least expensive brand of number 20 biscuits on hand. You will find yourself using many

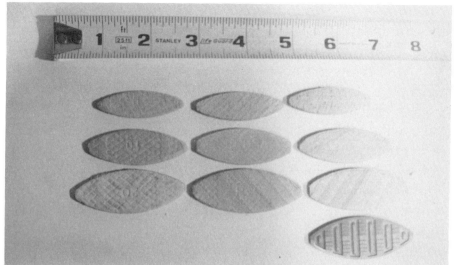

Illus. 3-1. A look at some of the commercially available biscuits. On the left are generic biscuits, in the middle are Porter-Cable biscuits, and on the right are Lamello biscuits. At the bottom right of the photograph is a K-20 clamping biscuit. All these biscuits are very similar, so buy the cheapest ones available.

Illus. 3-2. A stack of biscuits like the one shown here is required for even a small project. It's a good idea to have a few cartons of biscuits on hand.

biscuits (Illus. 3-2), and, if you do not live in the city, you will most likely not be able to buy the biscuits from your local hardware dealer. I telephoned my first order for biscuits to a company that advertised the best price; that company supplied biscuits in less than a week, which was good service. However, if you need the biscuits desperately, this could be far too long.

When you get the biscuits home, store them in sealed containers (for example, Ziplock bags) because they are affected by humidity. Improper storage could be expensive, since the biscuits cost as much as 3 cents apiece. Some biscuits fit very tightly when they are first inserted, and if they are stored improperly they can swell and become very difficult to insert.

After reading articles about drying carved stock in a microwave oven, I considered the possibility that biscuits that have swelled could be reused after they have been microwaved. Perhaps it is a matter of figuring out how much moisture leaves the biscuits in a certain period of time at a certain wattage, and determining how much the biscuit shrinks. Then, after making the calculations and microwaving the biscuits, the next step would probably be to compress them in a vise or strike them with a hammer to return them to a dry size so they can be used. Perhaps it might be easier to go over them lightly with a disc sander.

After all these steps, would the biscuits work as well the second time? Since a half box of biscuits represents an expense small shop owners can't overlook, I decided that it was worth an hour of experimentation to find out. After using a biscuit to set the dial indicator on my moisture meter at zero, I wet a biscuit and watched it expand by .015 inch over a period of approximately 10 minutes; then I microwaved it for 90 seconds on "high," moving it every 30 seconds. Each time I moved it, there was a biscuit-shaped "puddle" on the bottom of the oven, so moisture was obviously leaving it. After 90 seconds the biscuit was quite warm, so I remeasured it. All but .003 inch of the swelling had vanished, even without compression. Rewetting the biscuit expanded it to 0.12 inch almost instantly.

The experiment was a tentative success. Illus. 3-3 indicates that biscuits so treated might be fragile compared to other biscuits. I was able to break this biscuit by hand, and I could not do that to one that hadn't been swollen and reshrunk. Keeping biscuits dry in storage is the best approach to take.

Illus. 3-3. This broken biscuit snapped very easily after my dehydration experiment.

Biscuit Strength and Effectiveness

The first set of sample joints generally convinces most woodworkers of a need for a joiner in their shop. Here is a test that will help you determine the strength of biscuit joints: Make a small panel by taking two small pieces of hardwood, jointing them, and cutting joining slots 2½ inches on center from either end, and another halfway between them. Lay a fair amount of glue down the middle of each piece; be sure to get some into the slots you've sawn with the joiner according to all the manufacturer's instructions. Slide in three biscuits and clamp the piece with a single clamp. Allow the proper clamping time, and you'll be surprised by the joint's strength.

When I conducted this experiment in a shop that was heated to only about 60°F, I put the clamped piece in my office so that the glue, ordinary Titebound, could dry. After only 10 minutes of drying time, I brought the piece back into the shop, scraped off the excess glue (which still had not hardened), and ran the piece through the surface planer on both sides. As I "stressed" the piece in my hands, I could see some glue working in and out of a snipe in one end of the joint, a product of hasty stock preparation. Of course, the glue hadn't set in 10 minutes at that temperature, and the joining biscuits were all that were holding the panel together.

Wondering what it would take to break the joint, I began to apply stress to the panel in my hands by flexing it. After I put stress on the board for five minutes at full strength, the joint broke—but none of the three biscuits broke. The glue inside the joint was still wet.

Illus. 3-4—3-8 attest to the strength of joints made with

Illus. 3-4. These two small pieces of walnut were biscuited together and then sawn open to reveal the mechanical nature of the biscuit joint.

joiners. Illus. 3-4 shows two small walnut pieces that were joined with one biscuit, clamped together, and then sawn open to reveal the "mechanical" joint.

Illus. 3-5 shows two pieces of maple, each 1 × 3 × 12 inches, edge-joined with three biscuits. These pieces were scrap from my very cold winter shop. I was impatient to glue the machined pieces when I brought them into the house from the shop and set them on the radiator for nearly an hour, a foolish move. The pieces began to crack or split badly, but I glued them anyway and let the glue dry overnight. Despite the serious checking, some of which appeared to run two-thirds of the way through the boards, I had to hit the pieces with a hammer to break them, and even then it wasn't the joint that broke!

Illus. 3-6 shows a butt joint that was sloppily made with a single biscuit; you can see where I cut through the side slightly. The joint was biscuited and glued in place without clamp pressure, and left overnight. The joint would not break under just hand pressure, but

Illus. 3-5 (above left). These boards began to check badly after they dried out on a radiator while being warmed for gluing. Note, however, that the biscuits did not fail, a tribute to their strength. **Illus. 3-6 (above right).** To break the biscuit that joined these ¾ × 2½ × 30-inch pieces, I had to put one piece in my bench vise and apply all of my body weight to the other member.

Illus. 3-7. A broken joint in particleboard. Note that the biscuits have remained intact while the sheet stock has been destroyed.

only after I put one piece in my bench vise and applied full body pressure (at least 190 pounds) to the other. Then, finally, the joint yielded, breaking the biscuit.

Illus. 3-7 and 3-8 show close-ups of broken joints made in particleboard. Illus. 3-7 reveals that the piece of sheet stock broke before the joint did. Illus. 3-8 shows how much of the sheet stock

Illus. 3-8. Another broken biscuit joint in particleboard. Note that once again it was the particleboard that broke under great pressure, not the biscuit.

clung to each biscuit in another forcibly broken joint. A lot of modern furniture is made of veneered sheet stock like this.

If you use biscuits, you will be virtually guaranteed extremely solid joining work. Noted furniture-maker Graham Blackburn even joins chairs with biscuits. Even load-bearing shelves such as those used for phonograph records can be biscuit-joined in place.

How to Use Biscuits

All joining biscuits are made of solid beech. According to Lamello, its joining biscuits are made as follows: Felled tree trunks are cut to length and sawn into boards, which are then cut to squared timber and dried. Then the material is sawn into laths, which are processed to plates on a stamping press and are then sorted, counted, and packed.

Lamello claims that its biscuits are evenly pressed and feature fine-ground edges, with ends blunted to allow easy escape of superfluous glue. The biscuits manufactured by other companies do not look much different to me except for the amount of the ends that has been cut off. Porter-Cable claims that its American-made biscuits have more of a bevel on all their edges to allow for easier insertion, but, once again, I have some difficulty detecting the difference.

Biscuits are used for joining surfaces, corners, and frames, and can be used in joints that are butted, staggered, or mitred. They can be used on chipboard, solid wood, plywood, or other sheet materials.

Biscuits work like splines and dowels as they help to line up

Illus. 3-9. You have about ¼ inch of leeway when you are aligning a pair of joints. This should be enough to allow for perfect alignment.

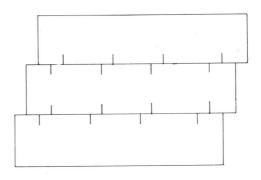

Illus. 3-10. Use a knife-like implement to remove the chips from the slots before beginning critical assemblies.

adjoining surfaces. However, they are preferred over dowels because they provide a greater wood-to-wood-surface gluing area, although you should use as many of them as possible since they are the only source of structural integrity.

When using biscuits, simply do the following: Align your cuts. Since the biscuit slots are cut slightly larger than the biscuits are, you don't have to line up your cuts perfectly lengthwise (Illus. 3-9). However, the joiner must be set up square or it may misalign the cuts widthwise.

When the slots are properly aligned and cut (Illus. 3-10), glue them with PVA (polyvinyl acetate) glue such as Elmer's or Titebond. Glue carefully. Dripping the glue down both sides of the slots (Illus. 3-11) is the best way of gluing except when you are edge-gluing or joining mitres. Just filling the slot can be too messy, and gluing the biscuit directly would dictate assembly times that are impossibly short.

The biscuits will get wet soon after insertion and expand, thus

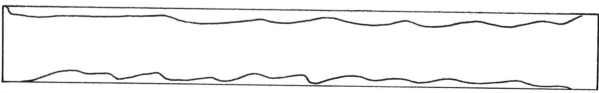

Illus. 3-11. Coat the sides of the slot with glue, as shown here, rather than let the glue pool in the bottom of the slot.

producing the required lateral pressure inside the groove. The continuous setting process of the glue leads to growing mechanical strength, which means that only a very short time is needed for clamping.

While biscuit-joining itself is very fast, take your time when cutting the members to be joined. Cut them very accurately and plan the assembly of your project carefully. A biscuit-joined project can be assembled much more neatly than any other type of project. You will find that you use far less glue, so the pieces can be all but "finish-sanded" before being finally assembled.

Accessory Biscuits

LAMELLO CLAMPING BISCUITS

The plastic, toothed, size-20 Lamello clamping biscuits (Illus. 3-12) are expensive. A box of these biscuits, however, should last you a

Illus. 3-12. Lamello K-20 plastic clamping biscuits are used with wooden biscuits for hard-to-clamp joints. Available only in size 20, a carton of these biscuits may last quite a while in your shop and help you to complete awkward joining projects.

Illus. 3-13. A K-20 clamping biscuit after it has been broken out of its slot. Note that the pliers and the ⅛-inch chisel required to remove the biscuit not only broke the biscuit into many pieces, they also damaged the slot.

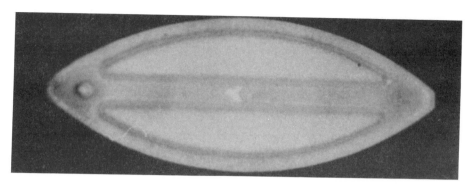

Illus. 3-14. Lamello C-20 joining plates are used to join solid surfacing materials that are being used increasingly for counter tops.

long time. You may not use them often, but when you do, you'll realize how valuable they are. These biscuits should be popular with all biscuit-joiner users. They are time-savers on projects that are too awkward in shape to clamp or on projects where even the neat gluing that one gets with the Lamello glue bottle isn't good enough. I installed one of these halfway, changed my mind, and then tried unsuccessfully to remove it with a pair of pliers. This attempt, shown in Illus. 3-13, destroyed the biscuit before it came out, and the attempted removal did the piece of particleboard into which I had half-installed the biscuit no good at all. Need I even mention that I decided to leave all future K-20 biscuits in place?

Illus. 3-14 shows a similar product—the C-20 joining plate—made exclusively for joining Corian, Avonite, Fountainhead, and other solid-surface materials that are becoming increasingly popular for countertops. These joining plates are made of almost completely clear plastic.

LAMELLO SIMPLEX KNOCKDOWN FITTINGS
Lamello Simplex knockdown fittings, as shown in Illus. 3-15, are made of aluminum and are expensive. In the right application,

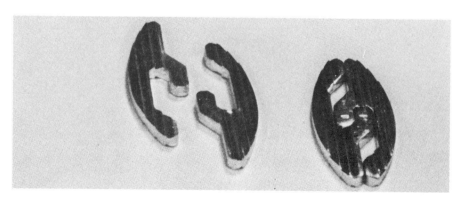

Illus. 3-15. Lamello Simplex knockdown fittings are made of aluminum. Sold in pairs, they are very helpful on items that must be quickly assembled or taken apart.

Illus. 3-16. A Simplex insertion tool and a pair of inserts.

they could be very useful. Sooner or later, we will be buying these fittings for frames, aprons, and other supports for heavy loads. One can even use them in tandem on a bed frame.

As with other Lamello biscuits mentioned here, you don't have to plunge-cut with a Lamello biscuit joiner to be able to use the fittings. Installation is easy: Simply cut mating slots, apply epoxy cement in both slots, and insert a connector in each slot. Lamello even has an insertion tool for this job (Illus. 3-16) if you want to ensure dead-centered positioning every time. This tool is certainly more of a luxury than a necessity; I have had great success installing these connectors freehand.

SKIL SELF-LOCKING PLASTIC BISCUITS

Skil 97704 self-locking plastic biscuits (Illus. 3-17) help wood-

Illus. 3-17. A Skil self-locking biscuit (left) compared to standard biscuits.

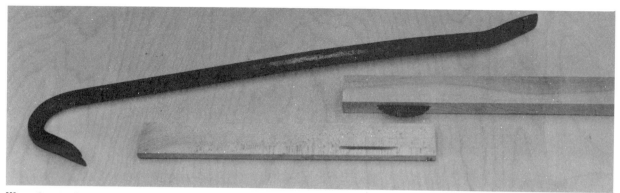

Illus. 3-18. It took this crowbar to finally break the joint shown here.

workers make convenient joints which are glued and force-fitted, but not clamped. The immediate advantages are reduced assembly time and joints that aren't affected by humidity. More important, these biscuited joints are essential in places where clamping isn't possible.

I joined two pieces of 14-inch-long maple scrap using one of these biscuits without glue; I had to force the joint together. I couldn't tear the pieces apart freehand, even though I used all my strength. Illus. 3-18 shows how they were separated. I was able to create an opening between the boards with a pry bar and then pry them apart. To remove the biscuit from the separated joint, I used a ⅛-inch chisel and a mallet, causing damage to the biscuit, but none to the work (Illus. 3-19). I then reassembled the same joint with the same biscuit, and again could not force it apart by hand. If you must disassemble a joint like this, use a narrow chisel rather than a pair

Illus. 3-19. Here a chisel is being used to remove the biscuit from a separate joint. Note the chips of plastic biscuit forming on the edge.

Illus. 3-20. Trying to remove the clamping biscuit with a pair of pliers didn't work at all.

of pliers (Illus. 3-20). The pliers will merely destroy the biscuit without removing it.

I used six Skil biscuits to mount a face frame on a wall-mounted hi-fi cabinet (Illus. 3-21 and 3-22) in my shop. This was a simple matter of cutting the width of the frame to match the width of the existing cabinet, marking the edges for the joints, and then, with the joiner set for the standard ¾-inch-thick operation, making plunge cuts in the edges of the cabinet and the inside face of the frame. After lining up the pieces, I had to drive the face frame home with a neoprene mallet. The glue set, and I will not be able to remove the face frame without a saw. Next, I hung the door on the frame. Once I clean the hi-fi, it should be able to run in the shop without attracting so much dust; this should reduce the need to vacuum it with accompanying bursts from an air hose on a weekly basis.

Less brittle and expensive than their Lamello counterparts, the Skil self-locking biscuits, especially when used properly with glue, make permanent joints. They are an inexpensive solution to many difficult joining problems, and I believe they should be your first choice in clamping biscuits.

OTHER LAMELLO BISCUITS

Until now, one disadvantage of biscuit joining was that the joints were always too wide for use with face-frame joinery. There are now biscuits available which can be used for face-frame joinery. One such biscuit is the Lamello H-9 (Illus. 3-23). These biscuits are only

Illus. 3-21. Six biscuits are more than enough to hold the face frame onto the shop's hi-fi cabinet.

Illus. 3-22. The face frame in place.

Illus. 3-23. A Lamello #9 biscuit and cutter (left) compared to a standard-size biscuit and cutter.

1½ inches long. Use them with a special cutter that will fit any joiner (except the Ryobi) to join picture-frame stock as narrow as 1¼ inches. If you do much framing, this setup is almost essential. These biscuits are also less than half the thickness of standard biscuits. If you use many of them, it might be a good idea to mount the H-9 cutter in a separate joiner. Before cutting, be sure to set the depth of cut to maximum (*D* on some machines).

Lamello has also introduced spline stock in two sizes: 13 inches long × 1⁷⁄₁₆ inches wide and 13¾ inches long × 2¹⁄₁₆ inches wide. This stock will be useful for joining material that can be slotted rather than merely biscuited, and it can be cut to the sizes needed (Illus. 3-24).

Other new biscuits are the #6, which is 3⁵⁄₁₆ inches long × 1³⁄₁₆ inches wide, and the #4, which is 2⅝ inches long × 1⅞ inches wide. Both of these are useful for joining extra-large material.

Illus. 3-24. Lamello splines latticed around a ruler.

Here is how they are installed: For the #6 biscuit, set the depth-of-cut gauge to maximum (*D* on some machines), make the first plunge cut, withdraw the joiner, move the joiner ⅜ inch, and plunge-cut again. When laying out the joint, mark both plunge points, rather than trying to achieve paired plunging by eye. To cut the slots for the #4 biscuit, first set the depth-of-cut gauge to *S*. This is a bit deeper than you'd cut for a #20 biscuit. Unfortunately, the *S* setting is not available on all joiners. Then make the plunge cut, move over slightly (⅜ inch will be too far if you want a precise fit), and plunge-cut again.

Before making cuts for either the #6 or #4 biscuit, make practice cuts in scrap stock, especially if you don't want the slots to be so oversize that they are sloppy-looking.

Lamello has begun packaging its professional accessories for sale in home centers and some catalogues. Now, occasional users can buy small quantities of standard joining biscuits, aluminum quick-connector biscuits for making knockdown furniture, K2 clamping biscuits for use on projects that would be difficult to clamp in more standard ways, and C20 plates for joining Corian and other high-quality, decorative synthetic panels.

Hafele/Knapp Biscuit Fasteners

According to the Hafele Company, what we used to call their KD (knockdown) fittings should now be called PAS (precision assembly systems) fittings, because they are used as alternatives to time-consuming gluing and clamping to make permanent joints. Several of these useful Hafele PAS fittings are described here.

Hafele/Knapp Champ biscuit fasteners (Illus. 3-25 and 3-26) consist of two pieces of precision-engineered, rugged plastic. Each piece is glued into a biscuit groove with common joiner's glue. Then it is pressed firmly in place with the template provided. You can easily cut the groove with a standard biscuit cutter using a #10 blade setting. You can also use a groove cutter with a 45-millimetre-diameter, 4-millimetre-wide blade. Once the glue has dried, either simply interlock the pieces for a snug, precise fit that can be readily disassembled or glue the pieces for a perfect and permanent fit. The Champ biscuit fastener tightens automatically as the pieces are pressed together.

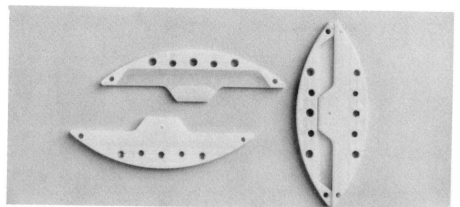

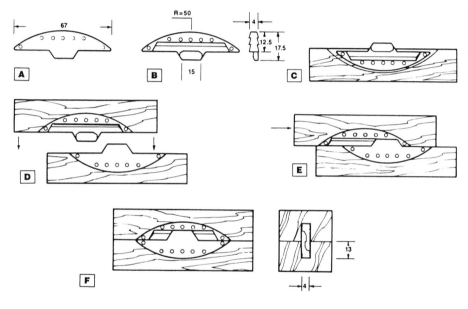

Illus. 3-26. Various views of the Hafele Knapp Champ fastener.

The Hafele/Knapp Metal fastener (Illus. 3-27 and 3-28) is an ideal connector for quick, strong, tight joints. Each section of a Hafele/Knapp Metal fastener is securely fitted into a 12.6-millimetre-deep biscuit groove and firmly anchored with two screws. The joint holds even heavy loads securely. Where needed, the Hafele/Knapp Metal fastener has the added advantage of locking the joint in one direction if you bend the flap bolt outward in the desired direction with a screwdriver. For pressed-wood applications, the joint should be secured with glue.

Hafele/Knapp Quick fasteners (Illus. 3-29 and 3-30) mount securely with just one hammer blow. You don't need clamps. You don't even have to wait for the glue in the groove to dry. This quick installation makes the Hafele/Knapp Quick fastener the ideal connector for a variety of applications, particularly door frames and other door fittings. Simply cut a groove using a standard biscuit cutter. Apply some common joiner's glue. Then, using the template provided, with a hammer instantly secure each piece in its respective groove. For a permanent precise joint, apply glue to the gap between the two connector pieces. The joint holds tightly and securely without the need for clamps.

Illus. 3-27. The Hafele Knapp Metal fastener.

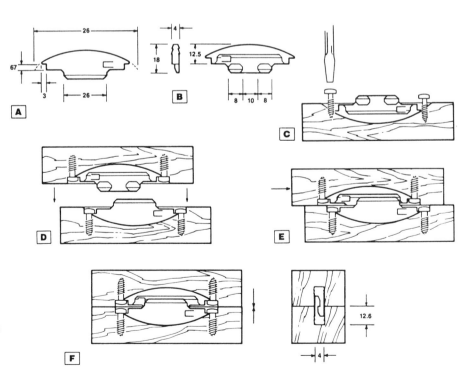

Illus. 3-28. Various views of the Hafele Knapp Metal fastener.

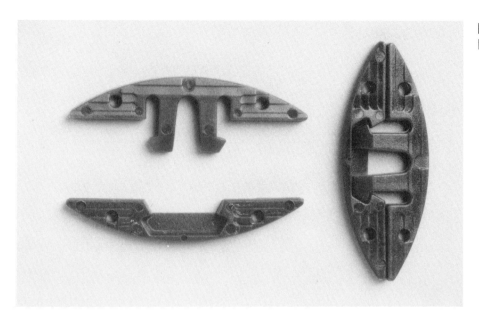

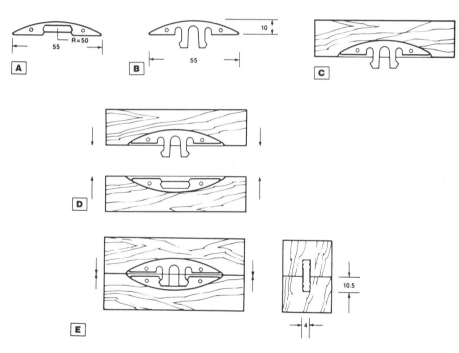

Illus. 3-30. Various views of the Hafele Knapp Quick fastener.

Hafele/Knapp Clip fasteners (Illus. 3-31 and 3-32) give stable connections at 90 degrees for applying mouldings and wooden borders quickly, precisely, and securely. Their unique bolt design make them readily adjustable for precise alignment. Mouldings or other cabinet and furniture components snap into place firmly. Connections made with these fasteners can be readily disassembled.

Illus. 3-31. The Hafele Knapp Clip fastener.

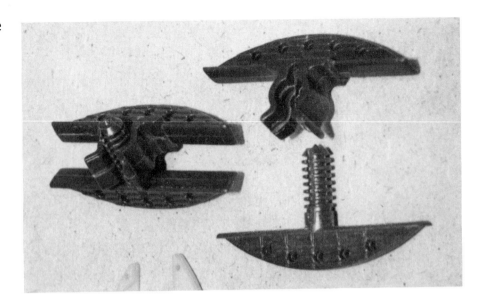

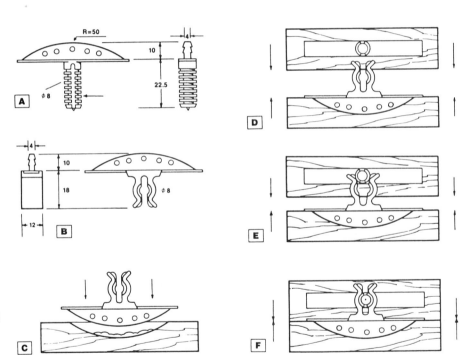

Illus. 3-32. Various views of the Hafele Knapp Clip fastener.

Maintenance and Cutting Techniques

4
Caring for Your Joiner: Maintenance and Troubleshooting

Many of us woodworkers are incredibly lax about periodic maintenance of our tools and equipment. Following a regular maintenance schedule is not just a question of keeping expensive tools working, but also a question of personal safety. Properly lubricated, sharp tools are safer than dull ones, because they do not have to be forced into the work by the operator.

Unless you are certain that you can put it back together without making a mistake, don't take your joiner apart. It is surely less expensive to pay an authorized service center to do routine

Illus. 4-1. Removing the spring on a joiner. Note the large hold-down clamps on the fixed-angle fence.

maintenance than to have to pay them to fix a tool you've reassembled improperly. Even after having taken dozens of tools apart, I am still apprehensive when I first operate a tool I have disassembled and reassembled. There are many things that can go wrong.

Check your tool's warranty. If the warranty is still good, return the tool to your dealer or factory-authorized service center rather than opening it yourself. Attempting to repair the tool on your own, even opening its outer assembly, will almost certainly void the warranty.

Certain repairs shouldn't even be attempted at home, but you should at least know how to change the blade and check the motor brushes. All the manufacturers specify that the second change of brushes (third set of brushes) should be done at a factory-authorized service center along with thorough cleaning and, generally, replacement of all gear grease. Let the trained technicians at these centers disassemble the tool when the brushes have to be changed.

To change the blade, do the following: First, remove the blade's cover. On the Bosch and Elu units this is a simple matter of removing a couple of screws or knurled nuts. On the other plunge-type joiners, you must remove the springs with the hook provided (Illus. 4-1 and 4-2) and the knurled nuts that adjust the depth of cut (Illus. 4-3).

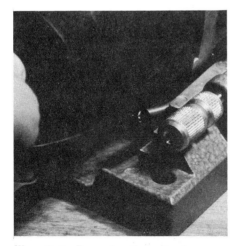

Illus. 4-2. Removing the pair of springs is an early step in disassembling the joiner.

Illus. 4-3. Removing the jamb nuts that adjust the depth of cut is another early step in disassembly.

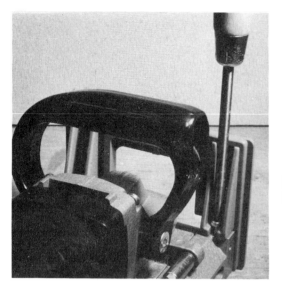

Illus. 4-4 and 4-5. To remove the faceplate, you have to remove this pair of screws.

After they are off, remove the faceplate from the slide assembly with a Phillips screwdriver (Illus. 4-4 and 4-5). Be sure to keep the stabilizer pins and their pressure springs in a safe place.

At this point, the rest of the cover just slides off, leaving an exposed blade. Remove the blade with wrenches or the allen wrench and spanner provided; these steps are shown in Illus. 4-6 and 4-7. On the units with a spindle lock, you'll only need one wrench.

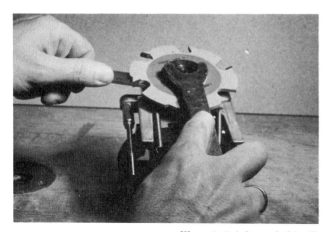
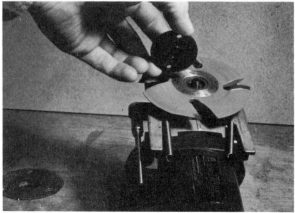

Illus. 4-6 (above left). Two wrenches are required for blade removal on all the joiners. **Illus. 4-7 (above right).** The last step in removing the blade is unscrewing this arbor.

On each machine, the blade is removed by turning it counter-clockwise. While the blade should require sharpening only approximately every several boxes of biscuits, this disassembly should be done fairly regularly for other reasons, like cleaning, oiling, and other fine-tuning.

If you have to disassemble the tool, pay particular attention to how the parts fit together. The tool's parts list is not sufficient to ensure proper reassembly. Here are the basic steps to disassembling the tool:

1. Lay out the parts in the order that you take them off the tool.
2. Remember how "tightly" each part is fastened so that you can return all the parts to the same torque. Where possible, use an appropriate torque wrench for this work; if, like myself, you don't have one, be sure you have a good memory.
3. Most of the fasteners on plate joiners are metric. Handle them with care, because they are harder to replace than inch-size fasteners. Use metric nut drivers and wrenches where needed; if you strip the shoulders off the hexagonal nuts, you will make it much more likely that next time you will have great trouble with disassembly.

Cleaning is an equally important part of the process. Be sure to clean dust and debris from the inside of the tool as you re-assemble it. The unit should be blown out regularly with compressed air (Illus. 4-8–4-10). Be sure to wear safety glasses while cleaning with compressed air.

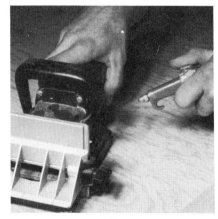

Illus. 4-8–4-10. The joiner should be blown out regularly with compressed air in the areas shown.

Illus. 4-11. Apply oil regularly but sparingly to both sides of the joiner's track.

From the slide assembly remove all traces of the residue formed by the mixing of sawdust and lubricating oil. Use toothpicks to remove small specks of this residue that are likely to accumulate in the corners. As you replace the slide assembly on the tool, lightly lubricate it (Illus. 4-11). This lubrication should be lightly repeated every few days or whenever the slide is not working as smoothly as possible, but not so often that the oil clutters up the work surfaces.

Motor brushes on the machines are all changed the same way. All manufacturers claim that the tool will simply stop before the tool's armature is destroyed by the carbon brush's spring. Ideally, this is so, but if the joiner is not maintained properly, this may not happen. Therefore, approximately every 50 hours of use, remove the motor cover, generally held in place by just one or two screws, and inspect the brushes. This should not take more than a minute, because the brush holders on all machines are easily accessible once the cover is off. Pay attention to the manufacturer's warnings and replace the brushes only with identical ones; to ensure optimum motor life, replace them in pairs (Illus. 4-12 and 4-13).

While you have the motor cover off, it is a good idea to blow the accumulated dust out of the motor. If you don't have a compressor,

Illus. 4-12 (above left). Sometimes you have to use a pair of needlenose pliers to completely remove tight motor brushes. **Illus. 4-13 (above right).** Shown here is the joiner motor. Note the partially removed motor brush.

a can of "photographer's air," which does not cost much, would make a wise investment. Another advantage to photographer's air is that there is never any liquid in it; liquid sometimes accumulates in compressed-air lines.

Changing the belt on the Porter-Cable 555 blade is a unique procedure. After you have removed the blade, remove the four screws on the base plate; this gives you access to the belt and pulley. Be sure to replace the blade with the exact-toothed "super torque" belt.

Following are some of the problems you may have to deal with when using a joiner:

1. Cord damage is almost inevitable in most shops. Replacing the cord shouldn't be difficult; remove the cover and attach an identical cord in the same manner as the damaged cord was installed.
2. A clogged dust chute is invariably the fault of the operator. After you stop the machine and unplug it, clean the dust chute by probing it with the unit's spring removal hook. Also, never run a unit with a chip extractor without also running the vacuum

cleaner; it only takes a few chips to jam the hose, and cleaning it will be a major challenge.

3. If you find that your unit is "skittish" when you cut very hard material, check your blade for sharpness and review your operating methods. Perhaps you should hold the tool more firmly.

4. If you have dropped the tool, check the slide assembly carefully to ascertain that it hasn't been bent out of shape.

Attending regularly to proper maintenance and storage is extremely important. Clean, sharp tools are safe, economical tools.

5
Edge-to-Edge Joining

While the butt joint is the joint most commonly associated with the joiner, let's begin by looking at edge joining, because edge joining generally has to be done before the panels are ready to be butt-joined. It takes only about an extra half minute per joint to cut slots and insert biscuits when edge-joining with biscuits, and the results will be a joint that will hold tightly without sliding around, and that will be flat and true even before you plane or sand it.

Illus. 5-1 shows the "poor" side of an edge-joined walnut panel on which no sanding, scraping, or planing has followed assembly; the only preparation this panel received was that the very narrow glue bead was removed before it had hardened. The arrows on the panel mark the seams. Very light sanding will make this panel as

Illus. 5-1. Note the marked seams in this edge-joined walnut panel. No sanding, scraping, or planing has followed assembly.

Illus. 5-2. Marking out a piece for edge-joining. I made the marks that appear on the piece more prominent than usual because I wanted them to show up in the photograph.

near perfect as is possible. The "snipe" at the top of the panel will be cut off. As you can tell from Illus. 5-1, when you have used a biscuit joiner, it is possible to achieve a smooth surface using a small but accurate surface planer.

To ensure the flattest possible work, glue only two pieces together at a time. Using this method, follow these easy steps for efficient edge-to-edge gluing as when making panels: Start with opposite sides of a wide panel, and glue two or three pairs of pieces at a time until you have one pair left, and then glue these pieces together. The layout is very easy. Mark the boards to be joined 2 inches from either end and about 8–10 inches apart between them. (Illus. 5-2 shows a rather closer placement, but 8–10 inches is almost ideal for edge joining.)

Edge joining is most easily done by placing the fixed-angle cutting guide or the flap fence at 90 degrees over the edge, as shown in Illus. 5-3, and cutting the edge and ends.

When edge-gluing panels, insert the biscuits about 10 inches apart. This interval is an estimate that is based on practical experience. In my shop, I tried three different biscuit placement options when gluing panels for a commercial project. On one pair of boards I placed a biscuit approximately every 8 inches; many biscuits were used and this seemed to be a waste of material. On the next pair of boards, I placed biscuits every 12 inches; those biscuits were spaced so far apart that the joined materials "wandered" and were uneven. Biscuits clamped at 10-inch intervals turned out to be just about right.

Biscuit joining like that used for edge-to-edge joining not only ensures flatter panels, it also allows you to remove clamps much sooner than you normally would. Since it becomes much harder to run out of clamps, your workshop will function much more smoothly.

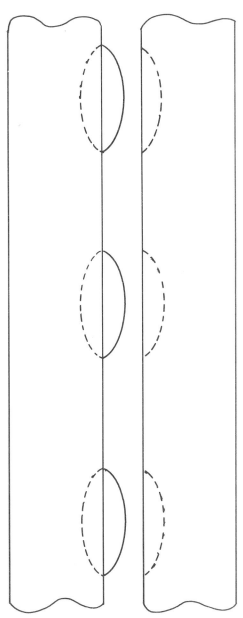

Illus. 5-3 (above). Cutting the slots for edge-joining in a small board. Boards this small don't really have to be biscuited together unless you have to use the wider piece immediately. **Illus. 5-4 (right).** When edge-joining, remember that the biscuits should be 8–10 inches apart.

6
Butt Joints

Corner Butt Joints

If joining joints quickly is important to you, you'll be intrigued by what you'll read here. Making standard corner butt joints is much quicker than dovetailing or dowelling.

There are two ways to make the standard corner butt joint used on internal members like partitions, dividers, etc. Both these methods will be described here. Decide upon one after trying both and use it, but not to the exclusion of the other. Each method has its advantages.

In both methods, accurate setup is the key to accurate work. The joint is laid out exactly the same (Illus. 6-2). Mark lines 2 inches in from each end of the joint and 4 to 6 inches apart between them. Make parallel rows (one or more from each side) if the workpieces are 1 inch thick or thicker. Layout is fast; the layout lines are only used to ensure that your slots are within a quarter-inch of one another throughout the length of the joint. After you have worked

Illus. 6-1. Butt corner joint used for framing work.

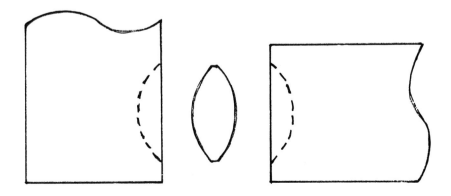

Illus. 6-2. A marked-out carcass butt joint.

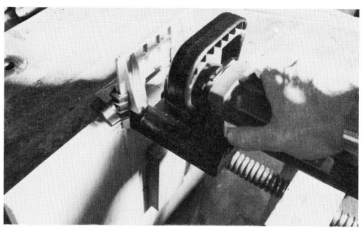

Illus. 6-3. The over-the-edge method of cutting produces results that are less accurate than those achieved through the second method.

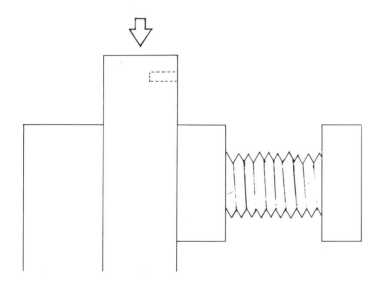

Illus. 6-4. In the over-the-edge method of cutting, the joiner rests on the narrow top edge of the board to be joined.

with the machine for approximately an hour, you'll be able to mark out your joints quite easily by eye rather than with a scale or template.

Next, cut the joints. In the first method, cut a slot on the face of one of the pair of pieces to be joined and cut a slot on the edge of the other piece (Illus. 6-3 and 6-4). This method puts the slots at an equal distance from the outside edge on both boards, which is exactly what is needed. The drawback to this method, however, is that the joint can get out of square if you don't cut accurately into the sides—which isn't easy to do.

In the second method, lay out a piece of material adjacent to your work that's the same thickness as that being joined. This material supports the machine as it works through the joinery. Stand the pieces edge to edge, perpendicular to one another; carefully lay out the vertical edge piece over on its axis, which is its inside edge. Scribe a line at that inside edge to ensure accurate positioning. Clamp the vertical piece to the horizontal piece so that the surfaces to be joined are at right angles to one another. Mark out the joints, again 2 inches from either end and about 4 inches apart in between. Mark out the joints only at the very edge of the "top" piece, as shown in Illus. 6-5. Using the extra piece to help support the joiner squarely (Illus. 6-6), first cut the vertical slots, as shown in Illus. 6-7 and 6-8. Then, after sweeping away the chips, cut the horizontal slots, as shown in Illus. 6-9 and 6-10.

Whichever method you choose to cut the joints, they glue up alike. After unclamping the pieces, put glue in the slots, insert the biscuits, and assemble them. There is no need to glue the end grain to the long grain, so it will pay handsome dividends if you do some preliminary finishing work before assembly. Glue as follows: Lay on its side one of the pieces that will carry the insert. Glue only the slots; either run a fair bead of glue down each side of the slot or use a plate-joining glue bottle. Insert the biscuits into each slot. Next, glue the slots on the pieces to be attached; then attach them immediately. Apply the next batch of glue and biscuits and finish the assembly.

Illus. 6-5. Shown here are the layout for a carcass corner butt joint and the shim piece (bottom) that will keep all the cuts square.

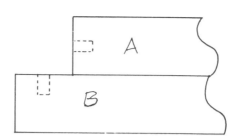

Illus. 6-6. The joiner rests squarely on the left block, C, while you cut A first, and then B.

Illus. 6-7 and 6-8. Cutting the vertical slots with the shim piece in position. This piece is slightly more difficult but rather more accurate than the over-the-edge method of cutting shown in Illus. 6-3 and 6-4.

Illus. 6-9. Cutting horizontal slots with the shim piece in position.

Proceed in this fashion for the entire project. Make sure that the assembly is physically possible according to the way you're proceeding. Test-fit the piece with dry biscuits before gluing it. Keep an extra 1,000 biscuits on hand. Even a very small project will take more biscuits than you have planned for.

Standard Butt Joints

Making standard butt joints to join internal carcass members (Illus. 6-11) is only marginally different from making corner butt joints.

When laying out an interior joint, as on a drawer frame, shelf, etc., lay out the joint to one side of the member rather than to its center (Illus. 6-12). In other words, if you want to center a ¾-inch piece exactly, lay out ⅜ inch to the side from which you plan to

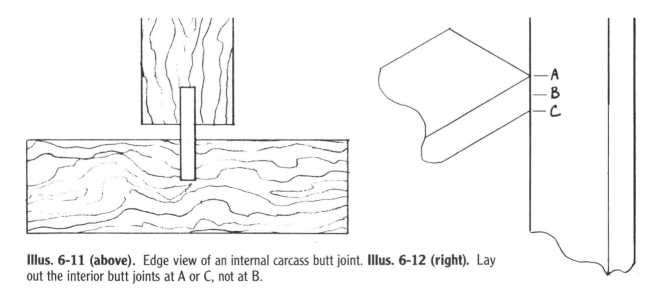

Illus. 6-11 (above). Edge view of an internal carcass butt joint. **Illus. 6-12 (right).** Lay out the interior butt joints at A or C, not at B.

work; this will produce a centered joint. The pieces must be laid out logically: Since you will be marking the sides (top or bottom, front or back) of the joints, use the same side all the time. Be sure to label where the pieces go; you will forget the assembly order, and that will lead to trouble, especially if you aren't cutting your biscuit slots exactly in the center of the work. As in the preferred method for the corner butt joint, first cut the vertical slots, as shown in Illus. 6-13 and 6-14, and then the horizontal slots, as shown in Illus. 6-15 and 6-16.

Making a small box is a simple procedure that integrates the steps described above. When using plate joinery to make the box,

Illus. 6-13 and 6-14. Cutting vertical slots for a carcass unit.

 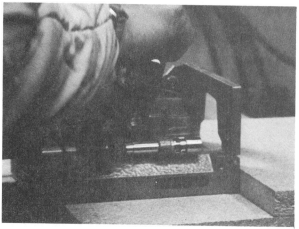

Illus. 6-15 and 6-16. Cutting the horizontal slots for a carcass member.

make sure that the planning and cutting are precise, which is the type of work that should be expected in a production shop.

Laying out the joints is the same procedure already described: Mark 2 inches from either end of the joint and about 4 inches apart between them (Illus. 6-17). After you have cut the slots, apply glue and biscuits to them, and assemble the joints as quickly as possible. Illus. 6-18 shows a carcass joint that was put together so quickly it had to be hastily disassembled for the photograph, which points out how well glue is distributed within the joint. Indeed, if clamping a joint should prove awkward, it can be held together by hand for about ten minutes. It took me less than ten minutes to join, glue, and assemble a small box from accurately cut pieces.

Illus. 6-19 and 6-20 show a drawer ring being slotted for mounting in a carcass unit (also see Illus. 6-21 and 6-22). Chapter 8 discusses how to make this kind of joint in thin stock. To make this joint in stock of normal thickness, again mark 2 inches from the left and right, and 4 inches on center in between. If there are many pieces, be sure to label them. Cut the vertical slots first, and then the horizontal ones.

Apply the glue and assemble. All the pieces that go between two other pieces must be added at once, and you must assemble the joint from the inside out. Failing to assemble all members that were cut from the same part of the logical sequence will mean you will

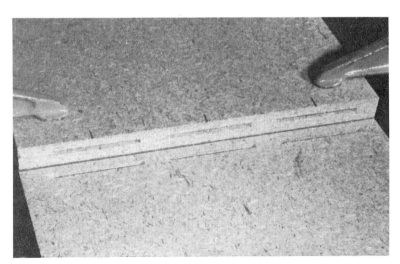 

Illus. 6-17 (left). The horizontal and vertical slots needed for this carcass joint.
Illus. 6-18 (right). A carcass joint with the biscuits in place.

Illus. 6-19 (above). Cutting mounting slots in a drawer ring. Note that the part of the biscuit in the joints that hold the drawer ring together shows, and will have to be chiselled or sawn out before the assembly is completed. **Illus. 6-20 (right).** Another view of the same cut.

Illus. 6-21 (above). Even though this small carcass unit has a lot of biscuits and slots, cutting and assembly were quicker than they would have been if another method of joinery had been used. **Illus. 6-22 (right).** This seems to be a very awkward way to clamp carcass units.

have to omit those parts; they can't be added in between biscuit-joined work.

It would be impossible to overemphasize the importance of partial finishing before beginning biscuit joinery, especially when joining these internal members. At the very least, sand with all but the finest grits of sandpaper. Assembly has to be done so quickly that failure to do the prefinishing will make some of the finishing virtually impossible to do—or at least painstakingly difficult.

After the sanding is done, assemble the pieces without doing any joining; the fit must be almost (if not absolutely) perfect. Correct any imperfections in the fit at this point. Then your finished product will be worthy of your signature.

These precautions also apply when you're making a large project. The hardest thing about making carcass units in a small shop is cutting the material accurately to both square and dimension. If you're working with expensive panel stock, it may be worthwhile to have your lumberyard do as much of the cutting as they reasonably can be expected to do—if they can do the cutting accurately.

Illus. 6-23 shows that even an extremely wide extension on your crosscutting gauge isn't enough for you to accurately crosscut or mitre wide stock. Even though the extension shown is nearly three feet long, it is not much better than the naked mitre gauge, which is not of much use. But if the extension has just been cut, as shown in Illus. 6-24, it can make a great layout aid if you can remember to tip it so that it is parallel to the saw's table as you measure over the edge with it. A better way to lay out the joint might be to add the thickness of the material you're cutting to the

Illus. 6-23 (left). No matter how long a mitre gauge's extensions are, it is not sufficient for crosscutting large panel members. **Illus. 6-24 (right).** A freshly cut mitre gauge extension can be a valuable layout tool.

width from the inside edge of the blade to the edge of the table, and then do your layout with a scale, a square, and a straightedge.

Instead of cutting with the crosscutting gauge in place, remove it (and the fence as well) and cut the piece while using a pair of 2 × 2-inch battens clamped to it as a fence against the side of the saw's table (Illus. 6-25). The batten should be at least a foot longer than the piece being cut, to ensure most accurate "fencing" jobs. There should also be a piece on top of the panel to keep the clamps from marring your work. Check with a square, as shown in Illus. 6-26, to ensure that you are working accurately.

The project shown in Illus. 6-27 and 6-28 was designed specifi-

Illus. 6-25. A pair of battens that will permit the side of the saw to serve as a fence is better than a mitre gauge.

Illus. 6-26. Make sure that your battens are square before you cut the large members.

cally to store some seldom-used writing supplies. Though the finished chest was to be kept in the basement, there were several requirements it had to meet: It couldn't take long to build (more than two hours was out of the question); it couldn't consume more than one sheet of material; it had to be inexpensive to make; and it had to be about the height of a table. All these criteria were met. This project was assembled with butt joints except for the top two joints, which are mitre joints.

Table 6-1 is a cutting list for this project. Techniques for adding a face frame are discussed in Chapter 8.

Illus. 6-27. A view of the carcass unit in its clamps.

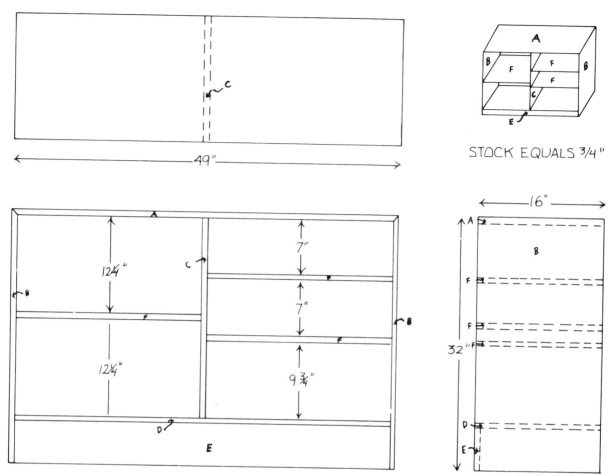

Illus. 6-28. Drawing detailing the parts and dimensions for the chest.

STOCK EQUALS 3/4"

		Cutting List	
Piece	**Quantity**	**Size**	**Description**
A	1	16 × 49″	top
B	2	16 × 32″	sides
C	1	16 × 27¼″	center divider
D	1	16 × 47¼″	bottom
E	2	3¼ × 47¼″	bottom supports
F	3	16 × 23⅜″	shelves

Table 6-1.

After you have cut out and mitred pieces A and B (see the next chapter), lay them out for joining. I used seven biscuits on each piece to join pieces E to D, seven more on each end of this joined unit to attach it to the sides, five biscuits at either end of C to attach it to A and D, five biscuits on each end of F to attach it into B and C, and five more on each end of A to mitre it to the corresponding pieces for B, for a total of 78 biscuits.

Before I had a joiner, I would never have considered mitring the top of the project in place. With the joiner, this job was easy.

This carcass unit only took approximately 90 minutes to cut out, join, and dry-assemble from the solid sheet. Disassembling it, gluing it, and reassembling it took another 25 minutes.

7
Mitre Joints

You can also use the joiner to make boxes and other carcass projects with mitred (Illus. 7-1 and 7-2) rather than butted corners. Fine European-style furniture is mitred and splined together, and now these kinds of joints can be made in home workshops with biscuit joinery.

Generally, we think of mitred joints as those cut at 45 degrees, so we will treat mitred joints of other degrees in the next chapter. The hardest thing about the mitred joint is preparing the stock for cutting the joint. Since the standard mitre gauge on a table saw isn't much good for crosscutting wide stock, clamp a straightedge accurately to the carcass piece and use the edge of the saw as a fence. This works well, but it provides ample possibilities for imprecision,

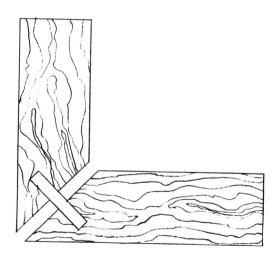
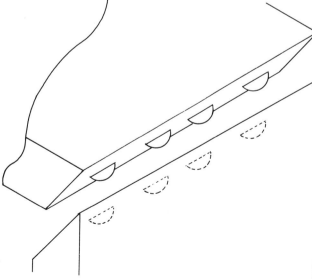

Illus. 7-1 (above). Side view of the carcass mitre joint.
Illus. 7-2 (right). A long mitre joint in a carcass unit.

and it is important that the pieces correspond to one another accurately if the joints are to work.

Following are the steps for preparing the stock for cutting:

1. Measure and mark (square) the length you wish to cut. If your setup is less than square and true, the results will be imperfect, but probably still better than when using the crosscutting fence alone.

2. Check the measurement from the edge of the saw table to the blade (on most saws, this is exactly 18 inches).

3. Mark 18¾ inches down from your cutting line (if you're cutting ¾-inch material; otherwise, add whatever is the thickness of the stock to the 18 inches) and clamp a straight board across the marks; check and double-check for square. I prefer a 2 × 2-inch board that is perfectly straight.

4. Remove the rip fence from the saw and make the cut using the edge of the saw table as a guide. This is much more accurate than using most mitre gauges for this kind of cut. You can square imperfect cuts by loosening one of the clamps and moving the batten ever so slightly.

After you have made the cut (Illus. 7-3–7-5), and the pieces are ready for joining, mark the stock on the mitred faces, adjust the depth of cut, and cut the slots 2 inches from the edges and about 4 inches on center between them.

Illus. 7-3. Cutting mitre joints.

Illus. 7-4 (above). Cutting a 45-degree joint with a fixed-angle joiner. **Illus. 7-5 (right).** It is better if you cut the pieces while they are firmly fixed in a vise.

The pieces are now ready to be joined. First, cut and fit any internal pieces for the biscuits, and then glue the whole unit (remember, only in the slots) and assemble it, preferably with a band clamp.

The Porter-Cable 555 is the only plate joiner that will accurately mitre together pieces of unequal thickness so that the outside edges meet without the need of a specialized setup (Illus. 7-6). The "extra" end grain is on the inside of the joint, where it is less likely to be visible. This way of mitring is substantially different from the approach taken by the other joiners. Other joiners have fixed angles at 90 and 45 degrees. All these joiners index their slotting cuts against the inside of the work. It is, therefore, fairly easy to cut either through the work or, worse, so close that exterior finishing makes the flaw visible. Also, unless the operator is meticulous, mitres cut with an inside-orientation mitre faceplate are likely to end up out of square somewhere in the joint; this is dangerous to the assembly, especially if you glue without first making a trial assembly.

I decided to build a simple compact disc storage unit, to hold my music collection until I could build a permanent unit. Below I describe the procedures for building this unit (Illus. 7-9 and 7-10), which contains mitred corners.

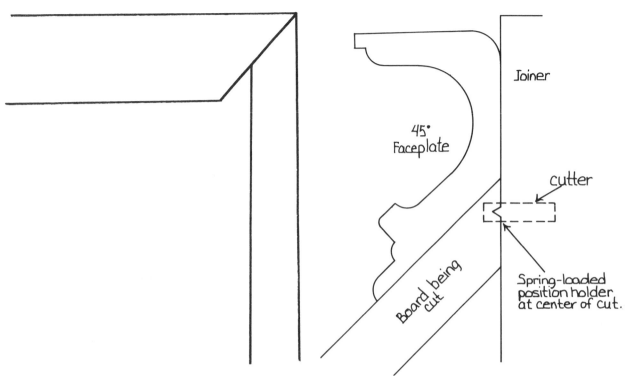

45°
Faceplate

Joiner

cutter

Spring-loaded
position holder
at center of cut.

Board being
cut

Illus. 7-6 (above left). The Porter-Cable 555 is the only joiner that comes from the factory ready to make mitred joints that meet at the outside of the corner rather than the inside. **Illus. 7-7 (above right).** This drawing shows the first cut made by the Porter-Cable 555 joiner in what well might be a double-biscuited carcass mitre joint.

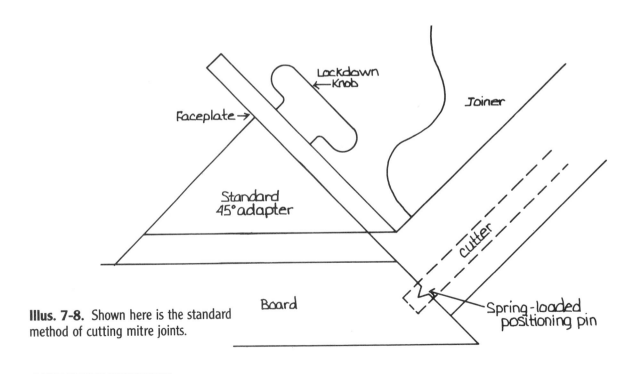

Lockdown
←Knob

Faceplate→

Joiner

Standard
45° adapter

cutter

Board

Spring-loaded
positioning pin

Illus. 7-8. Shown here is the standard method of cutting mitre joints.

Illus. 7-9. The completed compact disc storage unit.

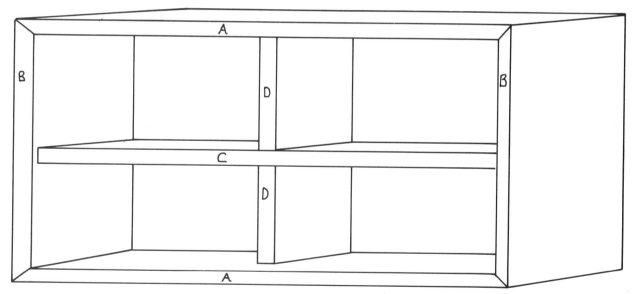

Illus. 7-10. Drawing of the compact disc storage unit.

Bear in mind as you read this description that the entire project took less than two hours to build and finish.

The first step to building the unit is, of course, assembling the materials, which are as follow:

Piece	Quantity	Description	Size
A*	2	top, bottom	$23 \times 5\frac{3}{4}''$
B*	2	sides	$12\frac{1}{2} \times 5\frac{3}{4}''$
C	1	shelf	$21\frac{1}{2} \times 5''$
D	3	dividers	$5 \times 5''$

*There should be a ¼″ rabbet along one edge for back. The A and B pieces have mitred ends.

After you have cut the pieces, test-fit the entire assembly. Sand all the inside pieces and the edges clean. Mark out all the joints and cut them. Cut the flat joints using the "paired" method already discussed. Cut the mitres all at once, using the joiner's mitre-cutting adjustment. Dry-fit the pieces and make any adjustments. Use the Lamello gluer; you will save an enormous amount of glue and cleanup time.

Use your imagination to adapt the unit to suit your own requirements.

8
Miscellaneous Joints

Cutting Offset Joints

Offset joints are all cut in the same manner as regular butted joints. Lay them out together, and then cut them with a shim in the joiner at one of the cuts. For example, the apron and the legs on a table sometimes aren't flush. You can set the apron back from the legs by simply setting a piece of ⅛-inch masonite or other appropriate shim between the apron and the height adjuster on the joiner's faceplate (Illus. 8-1–8-3).

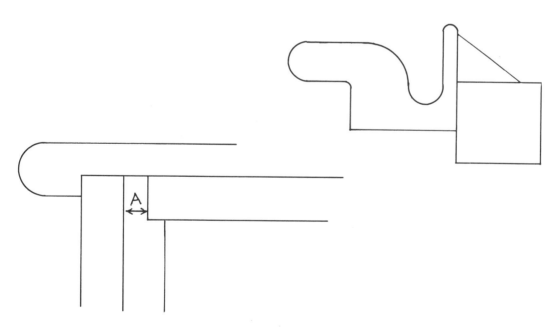

Illus. 8-1 (above left). A table-leg apron joint is a perfect example of an offset joint cut with a shim. **Illus. 8-2 (above right).** Cut the leg in the regular fashion.

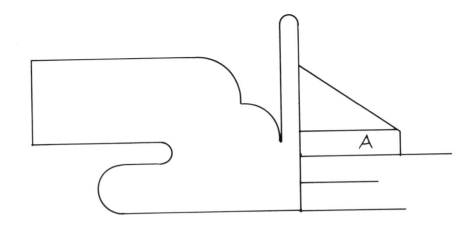

Illus. 8-3. With shim A equal to the offset shown in Illus. 8-1, cut the apron. On assembly, the fit will be offset perfectly.

Laying Out Narrow Work

You can lay out narrow pieces sometimes without even marking the work; the guide marks on the machine will show the outer limits of the workpiece and permit you to center the piece quickly using only your eyes (Illus. 8-4).

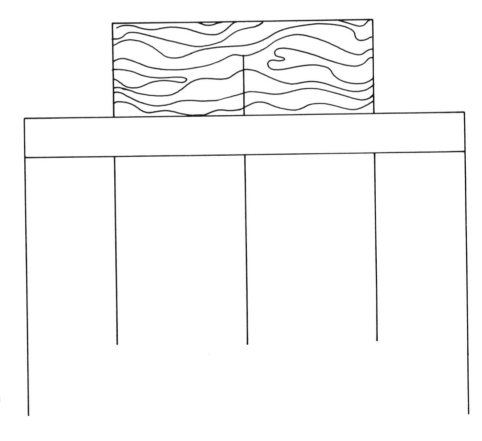

Illus. 8-4. Lay out the narrow work with the guide marks on the bottom of the joiner.

Cutting Joints at Nonstandard Angles

Joints other than 45- or 90-degree joints can be cut almost as easily as they. Cutting these joints is simply a matter of making an appropriate shim and fastening it to the fence of your joiner. Hot glue and duct tape work quite well for this fastening (Illus. 8-5), but you may want to screw these shims in place if you have many such joints to cut.

The shims should be about the same size as the face of your fixed-angle faceplate, generally about 2×5 inches, and can be attached to either the square or mitre face, whichever you find easier and more accurate. After you have removed the shim that has been glued and taped, you'll find that cleanup is surprisingly easy.

Illus. 8-5. Shown here is all the equipment needed to mount the various angle blocks. Clockwise from the top are the following: duct tape, the shop-made angle blocks, the fixed-angle faceplate, and a glue gun.

Illus. 8-6 and 8-7 show the making of a nonstandard-angle joint: A 15-degree shim is taped to the square side of the fence to make a 30-degree joint. While you could also tape it to the mitre face, doing it this way creates a "gap-proof" cut. This taped-on gauge was adjusted for this application simply by setting the front of it on the bench and then screwing it into place. This is a simple joint, but it can be used in a lot of applications.

Making Face-Frame Joints

Kitchen cabinetmakers, among other sheet stock users, will find the joiner useful for making the joint that attaches the hardwood face frame to the carcass, which was probably made of plywood. To set up for a face-frame joint, make jig blocks as wide as the offset shoulder, as shown in Illus. 8-8. This block is the basic setup for the entire operation.

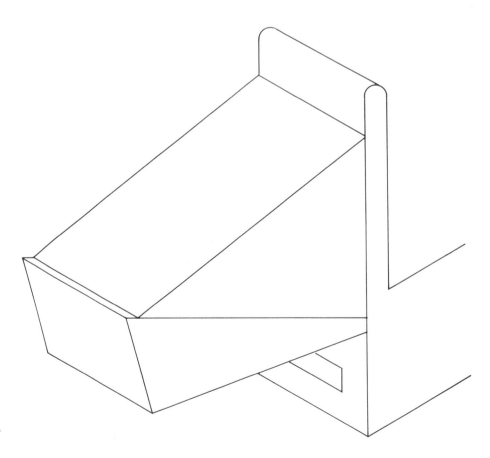

Illus. 8-6. To cut at a nonstandard angle, mount an angled shim on the bottom of the joiner.

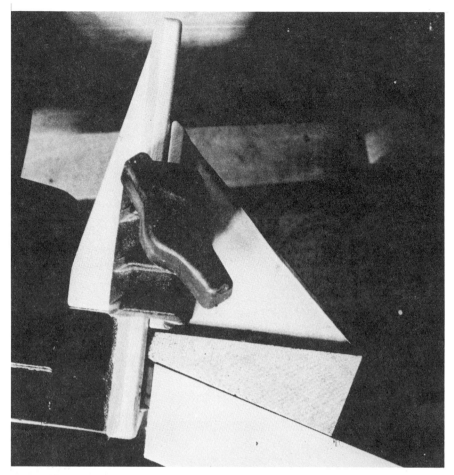

Illus. 8-7. Cutting at a nonstandard angle with a fixed-angle joiner and a shop-made shim. Note that the shim could be applied to the joiner either way, but the cuts tend to fit better when they are made this way.

Illus. 8-8 (below). Laying out a simple face-frame joint.

Make the cuts in the frame piece with the joiner resting on its base against this jig block, as in Illus. 8-9, and then cut the face piece with the fence resting on the edge, as in Illus. 8-10. Illus. 8-11 illustrates the perfect centering that this technique delivers.

Illus. 8-9. Making the carcass end of the face-frame joint.

Illus. 8-10. Cutting the groove in the back side of the face-frame joint.

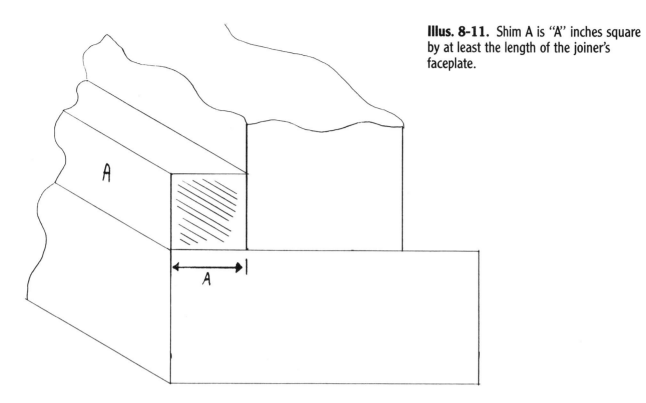

Illus. 8-11. Shim A is "A" inches square by at least the length of the joiner's faceplate.

9
Shop-Made Accessories

Filed Fixed-Angle Faceplate

Since I am advocating cutting mitres and nonstandard joints with jigs set up to cut from the outside of the joint rather than the inside, thus preventing gaps in the joints, the easiest shop-made jig to use is the Porter-Cable fixed-angle faceplate, filed judiciously to fit standard joiners. Illus. 9-1 shows this plate fitted to a Lamello joiner.

Illus. 9-1. After some judicious filing, the Porter-Cable fixed-angle faceplate can be fitted to this joiner and, no doubt, other joiners. This inexpensive part might be a desirable attachment for your joiners.

A flap-front faceplate does hold an advantage over the fixed-angle faceplate: It can be set square without a square. The only ways to set a fixed-angle faceplate are either with a square or by positioning the tool on a surface with a "square" piece of the right size to measure against; in each case, the built-in square marker is inadequate. The prototype for the Porter-Cable fixed-angle faceplate has a built-in square marker. I have a joiner like this that is about $\frac{1}{32}$ inch out of square, probably because of a misplaced screw hole.

Perhaps a better approach than adapting Porter-Cable's mitring fixture to your flap-front machine is cutting out a $2 \times 2 \times 5$-inch, 45-degree shim and attaching it to the flap front with two sheet-metal screws (through existing holes). With this jig, you can cut 0–45-degree mitres from the outside of the board rather than the inside (Illus. 9-2 and 9-3).

Illus. 9-2. A joiner with the shop-made angle-setting jig in place. Note that this jig may sometimes be preferable to the flap front in that it cuts the angle joints from the outside of the joint rather than the inside.

Illus. 9-3. Here is the joiner shown in Illus. 9-2 set up to cut mitres from the outside of the board at any angle. Now, if only there were a way to move the hinge on the joiner's front up and down.

Gauge Blocks

A set of gauge blocks for wood of the most common thicknesses will save you a great deal of time. Loosen the adjustable faceplate, and set it on the gauge with the base of the joiner flat on the bench. These gauges are better to use than the joiner's "square" slides because the slots on the mating pieces must be exactly parallel. This set of blocks will also make it easier to set up the tool for stacking biscuits when you need extra mechanical strength in the joint, particularly when joining thicker stock.

The blocks should be about 2 × 7 inches, so that they can be big enough to fully support the fixed-angle faceplate and still leave its label exposed; the label shows the measurement of the block. My set of blocks runs by sixteenths of an inch from ⅛ to ⅞ inch thick, with a block of Baltic birch included for good measure (my lumber dealer supplies this stock as ½ inch thick, but it isn't). The blocks can be combined for thicker pieces or you can choose various-sized blocks when you want to stagger biscuits in a joint that will be heavily stressed (Illus. 9-4 and 9-5).

Illus. 9-4. This partial collection of depth-adjusting blocks is shown in front of a joiner with a fixed-angle faceplate.

Illus. 9-5. A depth-adjusting block in place on a joiner with a fixed-angle faceplate.

Fixed-Angle Fence and Joining Table

The May/June 1987 issue of *Fine Woodworking* features an article by Graham Blackburn called "Plate Joinery: It's Strong Enough for Chairs." From the perspective of one who has never made a chair, I found the most interesting feature of the article to be his description of a jig he made for his Virutex O-81 joiner, which has since been discontinued. The standard joiner has a fixed-angle fence to control the location of the slot. This fixed-angle fence can be moved up and down, thereby allowing the blade to enter the work at varying points within the stock thickness, an absolute necessity when you want parallel rows of biscuits in a joint. The stand Blackburn fabricated for this unit was really just an extension of the tool's fixed-angle fence. The table was made of particleboard covered with plastic laminate and was screwed right to the fence. The entire setup could be clamped to the benchtop, so the work could be brought to the tool rather than the tool to the work. This simple adaptation made it possible to safely biscuit-join pieces that would otherwise be too small to hold securely.

With this setup, all sorts of shapes and sizes can be accommodated by clamping stops and blocks to the table. When the work is fed into the cutter against the machine's spring-loaded mechanism, the entire 12 × 16-inch table moves. To make angled joints, simply add wedges to raise or lower the workpiece's angle of approach to the blade before you clamp the workpiece to your table.

Blackburn's next step was to ensure a strong joint. He achieved this by using two biscuits per joint, positioning them side-by-side like twin tenons and thereby doubling the effective side-grain gluing surface. Since the plates would fit perfectly in their machined slots, the chances of a weak joint due to a poor fit were virtually eliminated. Almost all the joints he made were offset, unlike the flush-surface joints of typical face-frame work. Adjusting the position of the table and the fixed-angle fence to which it's attached took time, but, once done, the speed, accuracy, and ease with which the joints were cut repaid Blackburn handsomely.

When I inquired of Graham Blackburn where I could have some photographs of this jig to share with you here, he reported that he no longer had the jig in question, having recently adopted the Porter-Cable 555 as his joiner of choice. He did report, though, that he missed the jig and would soon be buying another standard plunge-type joiner for exclusive use with such a jig. Thus, Illus. 9-6 and 9-7 show not his implementation, but rather my very quick adaptation of his method. I made a 12 × 16-inch table as he did, routed a notch to fit the joiner's fixed-angle faceplate into, and determined where the screws would go to hold it in place; at that point I decided that a layer of sandpaper—about 120 grit—would be superior, for my applications anyway, to the plastic laminate that Blackburn used, at least in terms of "gripping" small pieces. (Illus. 9-6 and 9-7 show almost the entire setup. They do not show the screws through the faceplate.)

Illus. 9-6. The Blackburn-style table is shown here disassembled.

Illus. 9-7. A joiner is mounted to the Blackburn-style table to biscuit small pieces.

As I tried to reproduce his joining table, it occurred to me that a nearly ideal table for such a jig would be the INCA mortising table, as shown in Illus. 9-8, optional with the old-style INCA table saws. Preferring a Delta UniSaw to the smaller INCA saw, I bought the mortising table for independent mounting. Now that the joiner has just about made small-scale mortise-and-tenon joining obsolete, I have adapted this table for slotting small pieces.

Nearly everything on the joiner is round, so one might at first be somewhat confused as to how to mount the table. However, it soon becomes obvious: Remove the handle and use it as a pattern for the front yoke of your table-mounting clamp. I like the handle off, as shown in Illus. 9-9, so much that I almost hesitate to put it back on; after all, it doesn't seem to serve much good.

Full dimensions for the pieces to fit a Lamello Top joiner are given in Illus. 9-10. Though the Lamello Top has been discon-

Illus. 9-8. Before this INCA mortising table was used with the joiner, it was used with the mandrel shown here and an assortment of router bits.

Illus. 9-9. The Lamello Top looks better — and works at least as well — without its handle.

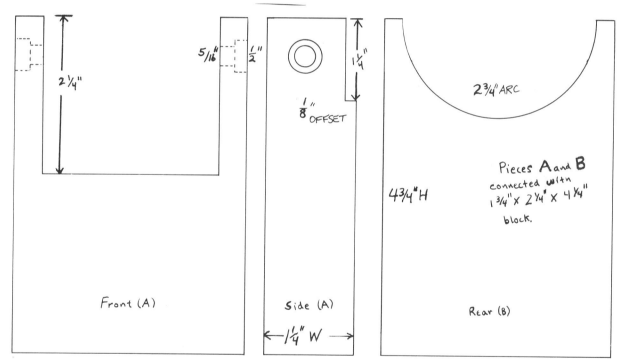

Front (A)

2¼"

5/16" ½"

⅛" OFFSET

1¼"

2¾" ARC

Side (A)

4¾"H

←— 1¼" W —→

Pieces A and B connected with 1 ¾" x 2 ¼" x 4 ¼" block.

Rear (B)

Illus. 9-10. The mounting platform for the Lamello Top. The Lamello Top has been discontinued, but you can adapt these dimensions for your own joiner.

tinued, you can adopt these dimensions for your joiner. First, drill the ¼-inch-deep recesses for the screwheads; then drill a 5⁄16-inch hole all the way through the 3¼-inch width of the block. Make both cuts a half-inch from the top of the block.

After the drilling is accurately done, cut a channel $2\frac{9}{16}$ inches wide by $2\frac{1}{4}$ inches deep for the joiner to fit into; it's better and, in the long run, quicker, to cut inside the line and file this channel out to width rather than leave the fit so sloppy that you have to start over. Next, drill the countersink and the hole for the $\frac{5}{16} \times$ 6-inch bolt that will attach the piece to the table. After inserting the bolt, screw this yoke to the joiner with the handle fasteners and mount it to the table. This block is shown in Illus. 9-11.

Illus. 9-11. This is the main support block for the INCA table when it is used for biscuit joining rather than standard mortising.

For the second piece in this unit, saw nearly half of a 2½-inch-diameter circle from one end, and then cut it to length at the other end so that the bottom of the joiner is exactly parallel to the INCA table. After cutting its countersink and bolt hole, mount it to the table. The unit is now ready to be used (Illus. 9-12–9-14). I found it necessary to use a piece of card stock to shim one of the supports to ensure perfect square.

This unit is made in such a way that the INCA table can be used with either the joiner or the mortising head for which it was originally designed; the changeover time is under five minutes, assuming, of course, that the needed parts and wrenches are immediately at hand.

Illus. 9-12. An underside view of the joiner/INCA table setup.

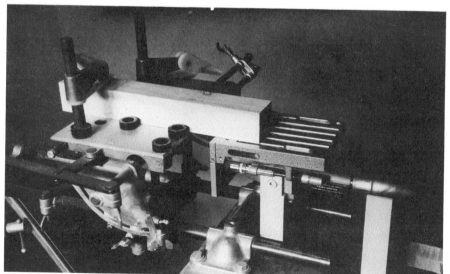

Illus. 9-13. The most important thing about the setup is that the joiner's blade must be absolutely parallel to the INCA table.

Illus. 9-14. The joiner/INCA table set up to cut slots in a piece of very narrow picture frame material.

It may be instructive to compare this jig to the Lamello stationary attachment used to mount the joiner to a commercial drill press's column. Of course, shop-made jigs aren't as sophisticated, but they aren't as expensive either. I mounted the joiner to the INCA table in under an hour with pieces of scrap wood; the net cost, excluding my labor, was zero.

Table-Model Biscuit Joiner

The shop-made table-model biscuit joiner isn't really an accessory, but rather a substitute for a joiner that was built in the days before a modest portable joiner could be bought inexpensively.

This table-model biscuit joiner is constructed by connecting a motor to one end of a pillow block mounted in a cabinet, and a saw blade (one that makes a 4-mm kerf and has a diameter of just over 4 inches) to the other end. The table is mounted on a pair of under-drawer drawer slides; a pair of guides holds it in place. Saw kerfs serve to mark the proper depth for size 20 biscuits; thin fillers could handily set up this table for size 10 and 0 biscuits. Sandpaper glued to the table holds the material steadily in position for slotting.

The cutterhead (Illus. 9-15) is covered with a piece of GE MARGARD plastic sheeting; this quarter-inch-thick clear plastic material is so hard it cannot be broken, even when struck with a pickax. It is exactly the sort of material you want between you and a failed cutter.

There are some problems with this joining table. First of all, there is no vertical adjustment. The cuts must be made at a predetermined height on the table. Second, there is no spring return to

Illus. 9-15. The cutterhead on the shop-made stationary biscuit-joining table.

Illus. 9-16. Another view of the shop-made biscuit-joining table.

Illus. 9-17. The outboard side of the shop-made biscuit-joining table. Note here the underdrawer glide and the cutouts that help control the depth of cut.

Illus. 9-18. Cabinetmaker Jon Jansen operating the shop-made stationary joiner.

help prevent the person from losing his balance while returning the table to its "start" position (Illus. 9-18 shows the operating pose this table requires). Finally, not all of us have access, as the fabricator of this table apparently does, to a never-ending supply of scrap parts with which to build these tables. Cabinetmaker Jon Jansen, of northern Wisconsin, who built the table, maintains that the box of biscuits he bought at discount represents fully half his cost for the device, including the safety features. By comparison, even the least expensive commercial joiner seems outrageously expensive.

10
Projects

Bookcase

Over the years I kept accumulating woodworking books and magazines that were too interesting to throw away. My shop became so cluttered I decided to build a fixed-shelf bookcase to store this material.

The main differences between building this bookcase (Illus. 10-1) with a joiner and building it by more conventional methods are those of time and convenience. Were I not building it with biscuit joints and mitred corners I would have to do the following: dovetail the upper and lower corners, add the base to the unit, and let the top shelf and center upright into router-cut dadoes in the underside of the top shelf. Cutting the ¼-inch × ¼-inch rabbet for the dust panel on the back would be more difficult, and I would have to rest the shelves on shelf standards.

Using the conventional method, I probably would have started without a formal plan, knowing that I needed a bookcase approximately four feet high by two and a half feet wide; the construction process would turn out to be more time-consuming, very frustrating, and not very efficient, though the results might have been very satisfying.

The joiner has brought efficiency to my shop. Here is the new, quicker order of construction with this tool. First, begin with a drawing; it doesn't have to be elaborate or to scale, but the dimensions must be right. Check and double-check your arithmetic as you make your cutting list. An accurate cutting list is absolutely essential to productive construction with joining biscuits.

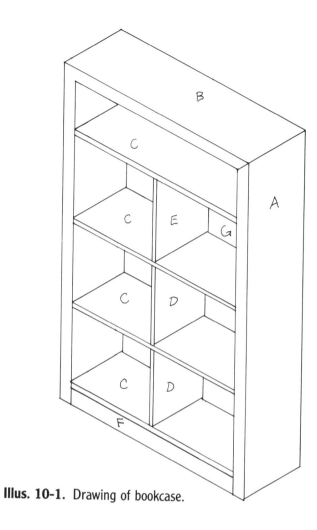

Illus. 10-1. Drawing of bookcase.

Cutting List for Bookcase

Piece	Qty	Description	Width	Length	Thickness
A	2	sides	9½″	48″	¾″
B	1	top	9½″	30″	¾″
C	1	shelf	9½″	28½″	¾″
C	3	shelves	9¼″	28½″	¾″
D	2	dividers	9¼″	11½″	¾″
D	1	divider	9¼″	12″	¾″
F	2	kick plate	2½″	28½″	¾″
G	1	back panel	29″	45½″	¼″
	46	biscuits			
		adhesive			
		finishing material			

Illus. 10-2. You can cut all the pieces exactly to length by attaching a stop to the crosscut fence of your table saw.

Accurately cut all the pieces on the cutting list in your shop (Illus. 10-2). If you are reproducing my bookcase, note that the bottom on one of the C members is ¼ inch wider than the others. Cut the mitres for the sides first. Then cut the pieces to length with the mitres meeting; this will ensure sides of equal length. Set the crosscut gauge on your table saw so that the piece fits exactly to the inside edges of the mitre joint before cutting the interior pieces to length.

Dry-assemble the pieces, adjusting them to get as near a perfect fit as possible. Make sure that the mitres you cut are square and true. Cut the rabbets for the back panel as you are cutting out

Illus. 10-3. Bottom shelf assembly.

Illus. 10-4. The bottom shelf ready for slotting.

the pieces; part of the beauty of joiner/biscuit construction is that you don't have to cut the rabbet by working all around the assembled carcass with a router.

Next, lay out the pieces for the biscuit slots that you will have to cut, always working in a logical order. The bookcase, for example, is best assembled on its side; after you have joined all pieces A and C in place, you can't join pieces D and E between them. The progression should work stepwise from bottom to top.

Illus. 10-5. Here is the bottom shelf with the slots in place.

Illus. 10-6. The layout for the next shelf. This layout continues in progression from the bottom of the bookcase to the top.

Because books are heavy, I used three biscuits per side on each shelf; two biscuits per end are sufficient to stabilize the spacers (C and D). Cut the slots with your joiner. The two kinds of cuts required here are for the carcass and mitre joints discussed in Chapters 6 and 7. Don't forget the single biscuit that joins each end of pieces F to pieces A; three or four more biscuits are enough to join F to the C you've selected as the bottom shelf. The layout takes just a few moments, and the cutting goes just as quickly.

After you have cut out the pieces and laid out and cut the biscuit slots, you may be tempted to assemble the piece as quickly as possible; don't. Before you glue the pieces together, do all but the final hand sanding; this will expedite things, for a 120-grit sanding belt can save time and produce good results much more quickly than 150-grit abrasive in an orbital sander.

After the sanding is completed, assemble the bookcase. First glue and fit pieces F to C; spread the glue into the slots, and run a line of glue between the slots on the surfaces to be joined. Use enough glue so that the surfaces join firmly, but not so much that you have a lot of glue to clean up. Some woodworkers prefer to remove the glue with a wet rag; I've always let it harden to at least

the consistency of cottage cheese and then take it off with a razor-sharp chisel.

Clamp these joints lightly and briefly. I've found that Weld-bond Professional Woodworker's Glue is ready to machine in 30 minutes, and when biscuiting I can usually remove the clamps in 15 minutes or less. Spring clamps with a 3¼-inch capacity are adequate for this job.

Even with the clamps in place, you can proceed to glue, add biscuits to, and join pieces C and F to A, which you're using as the bottom. Then glue and add biscuits to a D and another C, and add them to the assembly. Next, add another glued and biscuited D and C, and then an E and the last C.

Glue, add biscuits to, and assemble the mitre against the bottom. Then prepare all the slots that will meet the "top" A piece. If you are working alone, it will take a bit of work to get the pieces to drop in perfectly, but if you have dry-fitted accurately, you will succeed. Using a carcass clamp, clamp the unit in place for a short while; if you are working and building a lot of carcass pieces, the Lamello spanner set will prove extremely valuable.

After allowing the glue to set, remove the clamps, scrape any excess glue away, tack the back panel into place, and complete your hand sanding in preparation for applying the chemical finish of your choice. I used two applications of Watco Oil and a coat of Goddard's Cabinetmaker's Wax on mine.

I built this bookcase so quickly that by Monday evening I had all my woodworking books and back issues of *Popular Woodworking*, *Fine Woodworking*, and *American Woodworker* stored away neatly. If a couple of hours will take us from raw boards to finished product, most of us are more likely to take on small projects for the home.

Small Table

A small table is always useful, and this one (Illus. 10-8) can be made in just one afternoon with only about five board feet of material. Since the project uses so little material and can be assembled so quickly, you can well afford to spend a few extra minutes choosing the right piece of solid or veneered stock for the top, and you should be able to shape a much more attractive lip for it than my drawing shows.

There are two principal advantages to making the table with the biscuit joiner (Illus. 10-9–10-24). One, the time-consuming mortise-and-tenon joinery where the legs meet the apron is replaced by biscuits, which are actually just as strong. Second, instead of having to choose one of the relatively unsatisfactory conventional methods to attach the top, you have the option of using Lamello Lamex fasteners; these fasteners are effective and portable.

As with all biscuit-joined projects, first cut your stock to exact size. The nine components of this table use so little material that you should be able to prepare the material very quickly.

Cutting List for Small Table

Piece	Qty	Description	Width	Length	Thickness
A	1	top	11″	16″	7/8″
B	4	leg	1 1/2″	24″	1 1/2″
C	2	apron, end	4 3/4″	6″	7/8″
D	2	apron, side	4 3/4″	11″	7/8″
	8	biscuits			
	4	Lamello Lamex biscuits			

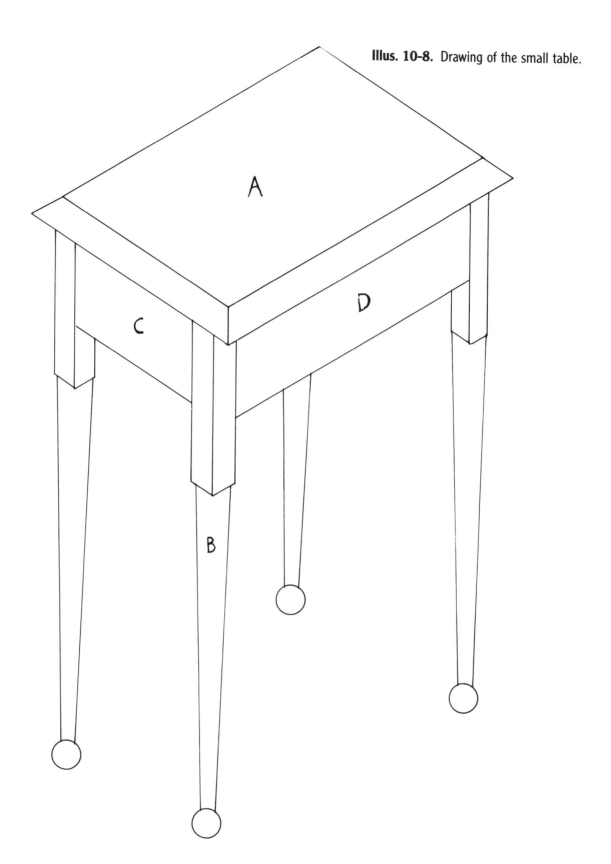

Illus. 10-8. Drawing of the small table.

Illus. 10-9. Lay out the tops, legs, and aprons of a comparable table project to be assembled. (Photo courtesy of Colonial Saw)

The legs on this table are turned, a technique that isn't discussed in this book, so we will assume that any turning or carving will be part of stock preparation. It may be useful to note here that the first 7½ inches of each leg is 1½ inches square and tapers down from 1¼ to ⅞ inches, with a 1¼-inch ball on the bottom. While I might have cut my mortise-and-tenon joints before I completed other stages of stock preparation in the conventional method, joining is so foolproof that you can groove the stock after completing all preparations.

After the material is prepared, mark the legs and aprons for tandem, offset biscuits (Illus. 10-10 and 10-11). Tandem biscuits double the amount of effective glue area, and offer an almost unbreakable completed joint. Cut first one pair of slots for each leg-apron joint (Illus. 10-12 and 10-13), using a shim equal to the amount you want the apron to be inset from the leg's front as you cut each apron piece; then readjust your joiner's faceplate so that the second row of slots will be about ¼ inch in from the first row, and proceed to cut the next round of slots, again using the shim on the apron pieces.

Don't glue the legs and apron pieces together until after all but final hand sanding has been completed. Then glue generously in the slots (Illus. 10-14–10-16) and very sparingly everywhere else. This leg set is almost too small to be clamped with a framing clamp

Illus. 10-10. Select the inside joining surfaces on the legs and mark the centerlines for the joining grooves. (Photo courtesy of Colonial Saw)

Illus. 10-11. Repeat the process for the aprons using the same measurements. (Photo courtesy of Colonial Saw)

Illus. 10-12. Using the center alignment mark on the joiner, plunge-cut the grooves in the aprons. (Photo courtesy of Colonial Saw)

Illus. 10-13. Then, while resting the joiner on the apron, plunge-cut the grooves in the legs, again using the center alignment mark. (Photo courtesy of Colonial Saw)

Illus. 10-14. For a permanent apron/leg assembly, apply water-based glue to the grooves. (Photo courtesy of Colonial Saw)

Illus. 10-15. Assemble the Lamello joining plates. (Photo courtesy of Colonial Saw)

such as those included with the Lamello spanner set, but it can be clamped quite successfully with small standard bar clamps. After the glue has set, remove the clamps and carefully scrape any excess glue away with a sharp chisel. Then, do the finish sanding.

To attach the top with the Lamello Lamex fasteners, set the top on the leg assembly and mark out the sides (long apron pieces) for a pair of biscuit joints. Cut the slots in the top and in the aprons (Illus. 10-17 and 10-18). Glue the Lamex joining biscuits in the aprons (Illus. 10-19). Following the instructions in Chapter 25, make the multiple plunge cuts to mill the wide slots for the Lamex fittings 90 degrees from the existing slots (Illus. 10-20). Use the Lamello hot-melt glue gun if you have the Lamello Lamex kit (Illus. 10-21), or epoxy them in place if you are milling these slots freehand.

After the Lamex connectors have been glued in place, attach the top simply by setting it in place and turning the four screws clockwise (Illus. 10-22). Of course, you can use the standard top-fastening techniques, but after you have tried the Lamex system, you will agree that it is a superior joining method.

After the top has been attached, give the project one last hand sanding with very fine paper (220 grit if you have sandpaper that is that fine) and apply the finish of your choice.

Excluding the scrub-waxing that was done a couple of days after completion, this project went from design to gratifying completion in a single afternoon.

Illus. 10-17. Position the base in the underside of the top. Then mark the inside and outside perimeters with a pencil line. Also mark lines for the joining plates on both the apron and top on the inside surface of the two adjacent sides and on the outside surface of the two opposite adjacent sides. Next, slide the table base back and to the side so that the outside perimeter line is aligned with the inside perimeter of the two marked adjacent sides. Clamp or block the table in place and, as this photograph shows, plunge-cut the grooves in the top, using the inside of the apron as your guide and aligning the center mark on the top with the centering mark on the joiner. Repeat the process using the outside of the opposite apron to cut the remaining grooves. (Photo courtesy of Colonial Saw)

Illus. 10-18. Using the right-angle plate on the Lamello machine, plunge-cut the grooves in the aprons at the center marks. Then cut the grooves in the apron using the inside as a guide on two sides. (Photo courtesy of Colonial Saw)

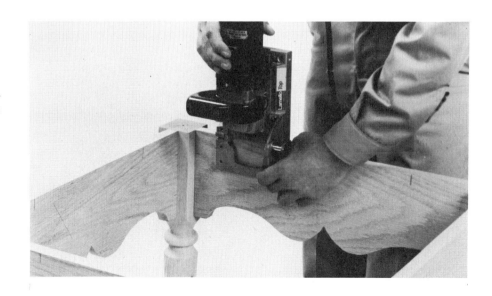

Illus. 10-19. Insert the Lamello Lamex joining plates with their holes exposed along the edge of the apron and aligned with the center marks. Allow them to set for 30 minutes. (Photo courtesy of Colonial Saw)

Illus. 10-20. To install Lamello Lamex KD fittings in the top, place the Lamex cutting guide in the groove, place the Lamello joiner in the cutting guide, and make multiple plunge cuts to mill the wide slots for the fittings. (Photo courtesy of Colonial Saw)

Illus. 10-21. Press the fitting in place in the slot and glue it with a hot-melt gun. In five minutes, the table, as shown here, will be ready for final assembly and finishing. (Photo courtesy of Colonial Saw)

Illus. 10-22. Mate the base to the top and tighten the Lamex fittings. Your table is complete. Assembly with biscuits was easier and faster than by any other method, and the result is a stronger table. (Photo courtesy of Colonial Saw)

Picture Frame

Making a frame can be simplified a great deal with the biscuit joiner if each piece is at least 1¾ inches wide so that the diagonal portions of the mitres will be 2½ inches wide; this allows them to be slotted for the biscuits without being scarred through the sides. Position the joiner carefully on this narrow work; cut slowly for precision. The slots will more or less fill these mitres. Cut the biscuit slots before cutting the rabbets that hold the picture and the glass.

Be sure to complete your sanding before assembling the unit; all you will be gluing will be the biscuits, since the glue on the end-grain-to-end-grain joint would be wasted anyway. Frame joints are at their strongest if they are double-biscuited, as shown in Illus. 10-23. The finished mitred frame will be much stronger and more attractive than one that has been simply glued or glued and nailed. If the frame is of material large enough to accept even a size 0 biscuit, just a single biscuit in each corner is better than cross-nailing in terms of the strength of the joint and the ease of application. Of course, clamping the frame with a band clamp like the one shown in Illus. 10-24—even if only for ten or fifteen minutes—is a good idea.

Illus. 10-23. This frame joint has two biscuits, a number-10 biscuit nearer the front of the frame, and a number-0 biscuit nearer the back.

Illus. 10-24. After it has been biscuited together, the frame should be clamped with a band clamp like the one shown here. For a larger mitred joint, a more substantial clamping system might be desirable.

Making a Drawer Ring

First, mark out the joint either freehand or with a rule (Illus. 10-25). Next, cut slots with your joiner; if the material is thick enough to accept them, two or more biscuits per corner are advisable because

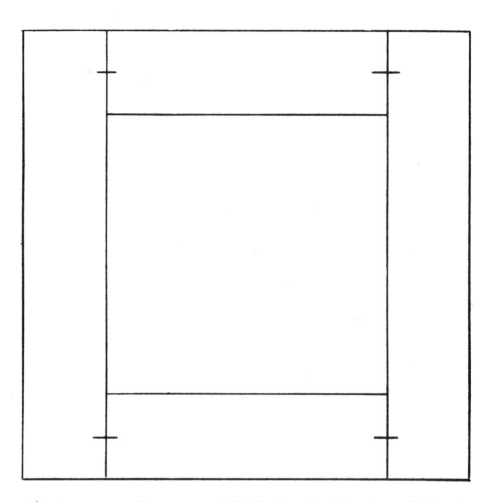

they are so much stronger. Third, glue the biscuits and joint in place; it is easier to remove any excess glue before it has dried rather than after it has dried. There will be some cut-through showing unless your side materials are at least 2¼ inches wide, but this really doesn't matter. Remove the clamp marks from the "good" face if you forgot to use the protective clamp block.

The piece is now ready to be biscuited into place. Use the procedures for the internal carcass member on the drawer ring (pages 56 and 57).

Commercially Available Joiners and Accessories

11
Buying Guidelines

The following chapters in this section describe joiners and commercial accessories available in the United States as of 1995. Manufacturers are continually making changes and improvements, so get up-to-date descriptions and price information from them. A summary of the units' features is provided on pages 220 and 221.

Don't buy a joiner sight unseen from a catalogue photo or a description in an advertisement. Don't even accept verbatim my descriptions of the models. Operate the joiner or at least examine it firsthand before deciding which model to buy. You'll have to live with this purchase for a long, long time.

The joiners available today share many of the same features. Many manufacturers, particularly those whose equipment costs more, do not like to admit this. The real difference is in the tolerances of the machined parts of these tools. These tolerances become progressively finer as the joiner becomes more expensive. I won't attempt to tell you whether the finer machining can justify the joiner's price: Only you and your credit card can make that judgment.

Until 1987, plate joining was expensive. That was because there were few joiners available on the market. The additions to the market since then have enhanced the selection you have to choose from, and there are many inexpensive joiners on the market.

What happens if (when) your joiner breaks down? After you've stopped cursing, read your warranty. Good help is available with whichever machine you choose. Some units offer a full year's "limited" warranty. The Lamello joiners, considered by some to be the very best, are warranted for six months. In any case, the best warranty is to ensure that you will not have to depend on one.

If after reading the following chapters you determine which

joiner you want, there are a few shopping guidelines you should abide by when buying your unit. Remember to operate or examine the unit firsthand. Also, I believe it's unethical to shop at a local merchant to get the feel of a tool, only to mail-order it from a discount store that can beat the local merchant's price. If you use the local dealer, you should buy your joiner from him—or there may not be someone to supply that information next time you go shopping. After all, your purchases provide those dealers' incomes. Now, I'm not saying that you have to buy locally—indeed, you may not be able to afford to—but it's not fair to expect the local merchant to provide the services when a distant dealer gets the profit.

When you get that joiner (or any other tool, for that matter) home, write the model number, serial number, and date of purchase on the cover of the manual. Then punch holes in the manual, and keep it with all your other tool manuals in a ring binder; my ring binder also includes sales receipts, repair records, and other related material. Keeping your materials organized thus ensures that you'll have them when needed. Sooner or later, even the best tools need repair. Keeping the necessary materials organized is but the first step in prolonging the tools' lives.

Now, on to the individual reviews.

12
Porter-Cable 555
Plate Joiner

The Porter-Cable 555 is the first American-made entry in the joiner market. This joiner has several features that make it unique. Its 5-amp, 8,000-RPM motor drives its blade by belt rather than by helical gear, so it's by far the quietest of the units (Illus. 12-1). With my sound-level meter, I gauged its noise level as 95 dB with no load, and 93 dB under load; under load it is much quieter than the next least-noisy joiner.

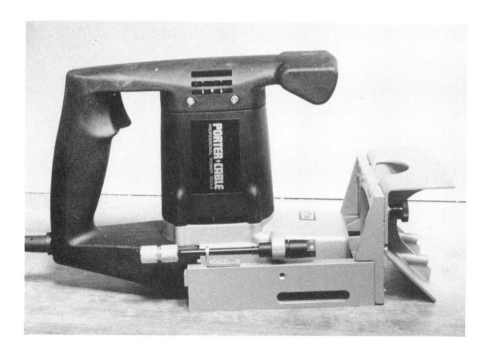

Illus. 12-1. This side view of the Porter-Cable 555 shows the workings of the fixed-angle faceplate and the depth-of-cut gauge.

This belt drive is not only quiet, it is also strong (Illus. 12-2 and 12-3). The joiner will supposedly cut 20,000 slots in oak without producing any noticeable wear on its toothed, "super torque" belt. While it might be a good idea to have an extra belt on hand, my own extensive use of the tool has produced no noticeable belt wear, so a spare is not really needed for the first couple of years of use.

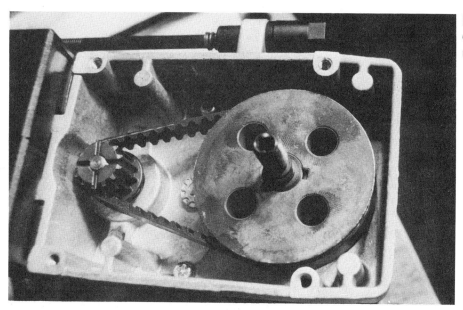

Illus. 12-2. The Porter-Cable's 555's drive belt is unique among the joiners.

Illus. 12-3. The inside of the Porter-Cable 555 joiner. Note the "super torque" belt.

Because of its radical design, the Porter-Cable 555 is not only one of the most comfortable of the joiners to operate, but at just under five pounds it is also the lightest. One could easily operate the tool all day. I have on many occasions.

Because it is so quiet and light, the Porter-Cable 555 is the safest joiner to use. These features reduce stress on the operator and those working around him.

The joiner's 7-foot cord is adequate, and its American-made metal case, shown in Illus. 12-4, may well be the sturdiest of the joiner cases.

The manual is a model of Porter-Cable's usual excellence in communication. In addition to the safety precautions that are common to all tool manuals, there are items specific to joiners that are worth reiterating here since so many of the other manuals omit them. They are as follow: The guard base must be kept in working order. Check its operation before each use, and do not use the tool if the guard does not close briskly over the blade. If the joiner is dropped, the guard may be forced out of alignment, thus restricting operation and making the tool dangerous. Keep the slide mechanism free of wood chips. Occasionally lubricate the ways with light machine oil, as this prevents excessive sawdust buildup. Keep the blades clean and sharp, because sharp blades minimize stalling and kickback. Guard against kickback; release the switch immediately if the blade binds or the saw stalls.

Illus. 12-4. The Porter-Cable 555 in its case.

Illus. 12-5. The faceplate on the Porter-Cable 555 is different from the faceplates on the other joiners.

The Porter-Cable 555 is different from the other joiners in that it indexes for mitre cuts against the outside of the work rather than the inside; this is what causes the Porter-Cable joiner to look radically different from other joiners. Illus. 12-5 shows the unusual faceplate. Illus. 12-6 shows the underside of the joiner.

Illus. 12-6. The underside of the Porter-Cable 555. Note the long layout line right up its center.

Illus. 12-7. The marked-out piece resting properly in the mitre-cutting gauge.

Mitred work should be laid out against the inside of the joint; the layout line corresponds to the long line down the center of the tool's bottom (Illus. 12-6 and 12-7). While seeing the work in this position may tempt you to operate the joiner upside down while squeezing the trigger with your little finger (Illus. 12-8), avoid this technique for the sake of both accuracy and safety. While the operation may be safe enough with a joiner, it could lead to unsafe

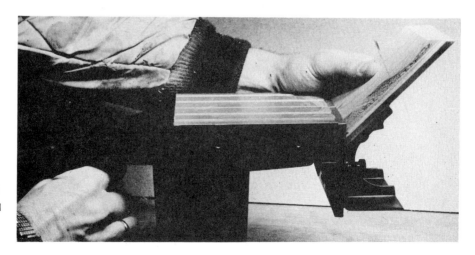

Illus. 12-8. For the sake of accuracy and safety, avoid cutting mitres the way that is shown here: with the Porter-Cable 555 resting on its top while you operate the trigger with your little finger.

habits with other tools, and safety should always be a consideration in the shop.

Illus. 12-9 shows the proper way to cut mitres. Mount the piece to be mitred in a sturdy vise. Thus, as Illus. 12-10 shows, when pieces of unequal thickness are mitred they meet correctly at the outside edge of the joint rather than at the inside edge.

Illus. 12-9. The proper way of cutting mitres. The piece should be held in a sturdy vise.

Illus. 12-10. Only the Porter-Cable 555 plate joiner will join mitres of unequal thickness so that they meet properly on the outside.

Illus. 12-11. This attempt at a storage case for small discs shows what happens if one doesn't set up carefully for mitre joining.

Because all other joiners join mitres by gauging from the inside of the joint, this sometimes results in either gaps in mitre joints or in the operator cutting the biscuit slot so deep that, after sanding, there are joining "blemishes" on the surface. Of course, you may run into the same kind of problems while using the Porter-Cable joiner (Illus. 12-11) if you do not set it up properly.

Though only mitring cuts have been addressed in this chapter, the Porter-Cable 555 is capable of making any joint that requires biscuits. Illus. 12-12 shows this machine being used to cut a T joint. This joiner offers an opportunity to quickly and efficiently make all types of joints, increase your efficiency as a craftsman, and perhaps achieve a new, higher level of quality in your work.

A note should be made here about Porter-Cable biscuits, which are also American-made. They are tapered for easier insertion and have notched ends. When you combine these features with the fact that the biscuits are considerably cheaper than the next least-expensive brand of biscuits, you can easily understand why they are so popular.

The Porter-Cable 555 has been vastly improved by the re-design of its removable/adjustable 90- and 45-degree faceplate. The faceplate on the original Porter-Cable 555 joiner had to be set with a square each time it was adjusted, because there weren't

Illus. 12-12. The Porter-Cable 555 being used to cut a T-joint.

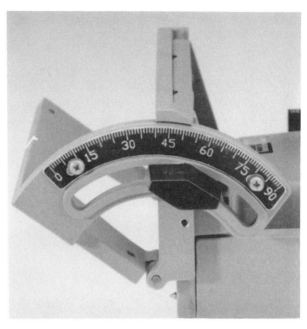

Illus. 12-13. The Porter-Cable's 555 tilt-fence accessory for a plate joiner.

enough large square edges to ensure perfect alignment. Now, a faceplate wraps around the sides of the fixed faceplate and rides the edges of the fixed faceplate squarely (Illus. 12-13). This faceplate permits the machine to mitre accurately at any angle under 90 degrees. These improvements have made this joiner the best value for the money. The Porter-Cable 555 is one of the tools that has helped make biscuit joining economical.

13
Elu 3380 Joiner/Groover

The Swiss-made Elu 3380 is a joiner/groover. Not only does it cut slots for biscuit joints, it can also be used for various kinds of trim-saw applications. This 600-watt machine runs at 7,500 RPM and weighs seven pounds. From two feet away, its noise readings are 97 dB (no load speed) and 103 dB (under load). Its cord is 10 feet, 7 inches long.

The Elu joiner has a momentary-contact-only switch, which seems to me to be the safest kind for most portable power tools. Its fitted metal case, with injection-moulded layout liners, is the most

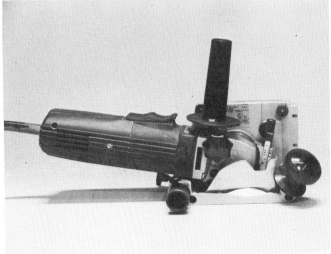

Illus. 13-1 (left). The Elu joiner/groover in its straight, upright position. **Illus. 13-2 (above).** Side view of the Elu joiner/groover.

Illus. 13-3. Despite its many advantages, the Elu joiner is awkward to use when its mitring attachment is in place.

compact of the cases available (Illus. 13-4). The manual, however, appears to serve the purpose of liability reduction far better than the purpose of consumer education.

While the joiner has not always been easily available in the United States over the years, it is worth noting that Elu is now a Black & Decker subsidiary. This is important, since Black & Decker will use its collective marketing skills to ensure a ready supply of both tools and service.

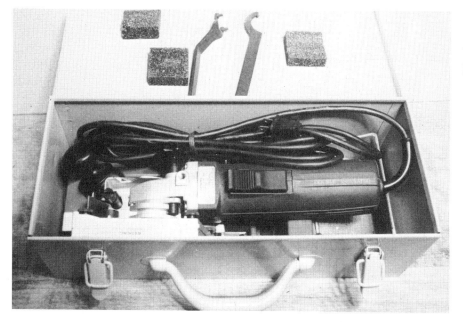

Illus. 13-4. The Elu joiner in its case. The bottom of this case is a piece of fitted plastic.

The Elu joiner is powerful and rattle-free. It features two operating positions, for it works as a groover as well as a biscuit joiner. As a left-handed woodworker, I have to say this model has the best chip ejector (Illus. 13-5). Unlike all the other joiners that shoot a lapful of chips at me with each cut, this one throws the chips away from me. Unless you are working in an area that must remain as "chip-free" as possible, this chip ejector may be even better than the dust extractors offered as accessories for some of the other joiners.

The joiner's basic operation is a bit different from that of the other joiners. The manufacturer claims that its primary function is to cut the recesses for joining pieces of wood and/or wood products using glue and flat dowels or biscuits, but its action seems at first to be a bit less precise than that of the other joiners. The operator must pivot it, rather than push it, into the work to get the plunge-cutting effect. To do this, hold the guard/shoe assembly firmly against the workpiece as you pivot the motor assembly. If you are less than perfectly steady or the work slips in its clamp, the well-machined base may move.

However, there is an advantage to using the Elu joiner. For easier access in tight situations, you can pivot the motor assembly

Illus. 13-5. Front view of the Elu joiner/groover. Don't be dismayed by the number of handles and adjustments you see. As you use the machine, you'll note that each one not only serves a purpose, it is also desirable. One advantage of this joiner is that it's the only one that throws sawdust away from the left-handed operator rather than towards him.

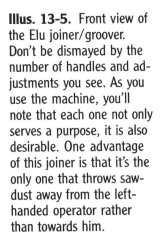

with respect to the shoe and guard by loosening the locking knob and rotating the tool to the desired position. Be sure to retighten this knob before proceeding with other adjustments.

To adjust the depth of cut, turn the depth-of-cut adjuster clockwise to cut shallower, and counterclockwise to cut deeper. The depth scale shows the depth the cutter protrudes beyond the bottom of the shoe.

For plate joining, the following sizing information is imperative: Biscuit size 0 is equal to 8 on the cutting scale; biscuit size 10 is equal to 10 on the cutting scale; and biscuit size 20 is equal to 12 on the cutting scale.

Side-to-side blade adjustment is not available on the other joiners to the same extent it is on the Elu (Illus. 13-6 and 13-7). Of course, all the tools will permit coarse adjustment with a fence, but the Elu additionally offers a fine adjustment by rotation of the handscrew at the rear of the main shoe. Turning the handscrew clockwise moves the blade towards the fence; counterclockwise moves it away from the fence. The manufacturer cautions the operator not to adjust the handscrew while the motor is running,

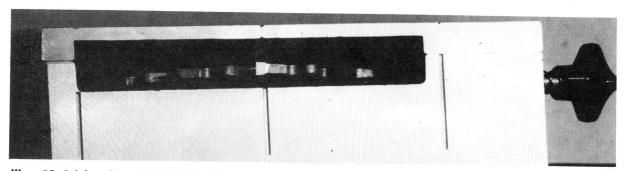

Illus. 13-6 (above) and 13-7 (below). As you can tell from the photographs, the blade on the Elu joiner/groover can be moved laterally nearly a quarter of an inch from the seam where the blade cover meets the base.

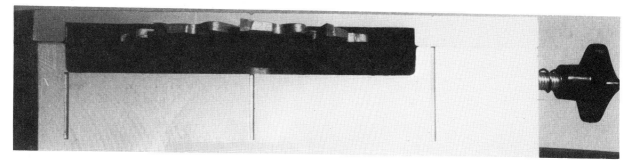

nor to adjust the screw to either extreme, as the cutter may hit the guard. I discuss this feature in further depth later on in this chapter.

As with almost all other joiner operations, try your settings on scrap pieces first. Mark the location for the biscuit recess in both pieces to be joined. It is usually easier to mark the work on the side adjacent to the side that is being slotted. Clamp the workpiece securely. Then, holding the joiner firmly in both hands, align the mark on the guard cover (visible through the sight hole in the side fence) with the mark on the workpiece.

Laying out joints with the Elu joiner is more similar to laying out joints with other joiners than I initially thought. All you have to do to join the pieces is mark the line on the higher of the pieces.

To plunge the cutter into the work, start the motor and pivot the motor assembly. As already mentioned, this joiner differs from the standard joiner because it requires a pivoting rather than plunging motion from its operator. At first this may seem awkward, but after you get used to it, it will not be a problem.

The Elu joiner's blade has 12 teeth, twice as many as most of the blades for the other joiners. It looks like the most substantial of all the blades and I've been tempted to replace the blade on my other joiners with a blade like this (Illus. 13-8).

The Elu joiner has a plastic anti-splintering insert, as shown in Illus. 13-9, which should be inserted when you cut into veneered panels. Assemble the insert into the grooves in the guard and cut a

Illus. 13-8. The blade of the Elu joiner/groover has twice as many teeth as most of the blades on the other joiners.

Illus. 13-9. This plastic insert fits into the mouth of the Elu joiner/groover to prevent chipping when grooving or slotting in fine veneers.

slot through the insert by placing the tool against a piece of soft wood and pivoting the cutter down through the insert and into the wood. The only problem I can see with this otherwise excellent accessory is that apparently only one piece comes with the tool, and the manual does not mention how to order additional pieces. I anticipate needing many more of these pieces.

Another advantage of the Elu joiner is the ease with which its blade can be changed or adjusted. As shown in Illus. 13-10, this is the only biscuit joiner with a blade guard that doesn't have to be removed with a tool. Of course, the blade has to be removed with tools (Illus. 13-11). A C spanner fits between the cutter and guard to the left side of the spindle and hook spanner into the notch on the

Illus. 13-10 (left). The Elu joiner/groover with its faceplate removed. **Illus. 13-11 (above).** Even though the Elu joiner at first looks very different from other joiners, when you disassemble it you'll note that it looks very similar to a 4-inch grinder — as do most of the other joiners.

Illus. 13-12 (above). An interior look at the Elu joiner/groover showing the main gear. **Illus. 13-13 (right).** A partial look at the inside workings of the Elu joiner. Note the motor compartment.

inner clamp washer; because the threads are "left-handed," you have to turn them clockwise to remove the blade. Be sure to check the direction of the cutter rotation when replacing the blade.

Because the Elu joiner angles into the cut rather than plunging straight in, this unit sometimes shakes when it is being used. Clamping the work is imperative.

This joiner is the only unit tested that lacked spring-loaded positioning pins or other means of holding the work while joining, and unless the grooving feature is important to you, this may be a major failing of the machine. On the other hand, if you could learn to overcome this shortcoming, it should be noted that the general design and construction of the machine are the best among the joiners.

As shown in Illus. 13-10–13-13, when the Elu is disassembled it seems to have more in common with the other joiners than originally thought. It is similar to a 4-inch grinder, especially on the inside. However, unlike the other machines, the blade on the Elu joiner adjusts precisely to the machine, or to about 3/16 inch to either side of it. This feature, when coupled with the fence, as shown in

Illus. 13-14, makes the unit handy for grooving. It also allows for fine positioning of the slots when slotting.

To fully appreciate this, you might have to experience what I discovered as I built a small compartmentalized box with another joiner. After the edge joints were cut and fitted, I started preparing the interior pieces for mounting. Here the trick is to line up the same edge of each joint, cut the vertical slots first, and then, after sweeping away the chips, cut the horizontal slots. The marking out is very simple—a few small marks are all you need to line up your work.

I discovered that the blade on the joiner I was using is too high for centered cuts in ½-inch stock; a standard joiner won't make this cut without a lot of manipulation. This is where a machine like the Elu comes in especially handy. I fastened a half-inch piece of Baltic birch plywood with biscuits on four sides. This plywood was ½ inch thick, and the other pieces in the project were ⅝ inch thick.

I positioned the Elu joiner's cutter exactly in the center of the half-inch plywood, as shown in Illus. 13-15, and cut a groove rather than just individual biscuit holes. This turned what could have been a most unpleasant repair into an easy job. (Remember when using any joiner that it is the operator, not the tool, who makes costly mistakes. Therefore, always measure twice, and cut once, and be sure that you have the machine's settings secured tightly in place.)

Illus. 13-14. Back view of the Elu joiner/groover with the rip fence in place.

Illus. 13-15. The Elu joiner/groover with its adjustable blade height can easily center a cut in a piece that will be carcass-mounted.

Once when I was using the joiner I noticed that there were too many chips on the floor and decided to start cleaning up. The broom I was using hit the cord of the Elu unit too hard. The Elu unit hit the floor—a fall of about three feet. There was absolutely no damage to the joiner. Kudos to the design engineers at Elu, who understand that we are now and again likely to drop a tool. Nevertheless, I hesitate to repeat this unintended experiment with the other models.

One improvement that I would love to see is a cordless version of this or any other joiner. A joiner that sits in a continuous charger while it's not in use would be ideal. The manufacturer who offers a high-quality version of this type of joiner will have at least one ready customer: me.

14
Freud Joiners

In the previous version of this book, I described the Freud JS-100, a relatively new, moderately priced entry in the joiner market. This joiner has since been improved, and a new model—the JS-102 (Illus. 14-1)—has been added. Both models live up to the manufacturer's logo: "*Precisely* what you need."

The Freud joiners come with an industrial-quality $3^{15}/_{16}$-inch-diameter × $^{5}/_{32}$-inch-thick blade (Illus. 14-2) with an anti-kickback design. A dust bag is now standard (Illus. 14-3); further, given a couple of wraps of friction tape, the dust chute would be a perfect fit for the Bosch AirStream dust hose described in Chapter 23. A six-position depth stop allows the tool to join with all currently available biscuits (Illus. 14-4). The machined blade housing is of better quality than the housings on many of the other tools, particularly those that are not metal.

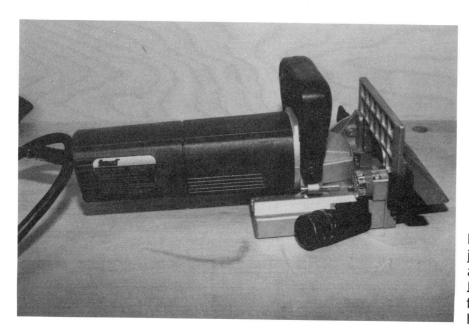

Illus. 14-1. The JS-102 joiner. The JS-102 joiner is almost identical to the JS-100 joiner. The only difference is that the JS-102 has a flap face.

Illus. 14-2. A close-up of the blade on the Freud joiners.

Illus. 14-3. The dust bag extends at an angle, so that it doesn't interfere with the positions of your hand.

Illus. 14-4. Notice the six position settings for the depth of cut, and the large, angled dust chute.

The JS-100 differs from the JS-102 joiner in only one respect: It does not have a flap face. The new model has been greatly improved over the original version. It is much quieter, and the holding pins on the faceplate have been replaced with rubber bumpers, which are more effective. The original had a three-position stop; as mentioned, the new version has a six-position stop.

The JS-102 joiner's aluminum flap fence is extremely convenient and accurate (Illus. 14-5).

The joiners arrive in a form-fitted case (Illus. 14-6). Though I have reservations about such cases, a visiting woodworker who helped me open the machine was very impressed with its case. The case contains the tool, all wrenches and adjusting tools, lubricant, and ten biscuits of each size.

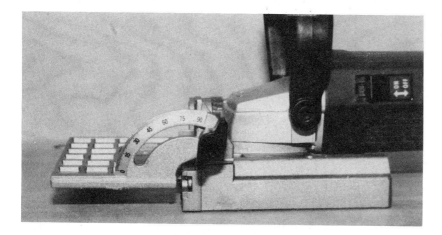

Illus. 14-5. The JS-102 joiner's flap face is terrific for working ¾-inch-thick stock.

Illus. 14-6. The Freud JS-102 joiner in its fitted case.

The joiners run at 120 volts, 5 amps, and at 10,000 RPM. At 6.2 pounds, they are relatively light, but still feel quite substantial. Their aluminum fences have inch- and metric-measure scales (Illus. 14-7). The scales are read against the top of the sliding fence. Every adjustment during use can be made one-handed. The joiners have 8-foot cords.

The tools are made in Spain. Freud supplies a one-year limited warranty.

Illus. 14-7. A close-up of the face reveals a pair of accurate scales for aligning imperial and metric cuts.

Illus. 14-8. Even a complete disassembly can be done very quickly.

15
PrinceCraft Biscuit Joiners

In the previous version of this book, I described the PrinceCraft biscuit joiner, an Asian-made imitation of the Freud joiner. That particular PrinceCraft model is now being sold under various brand names such as AMT.

There is a new joiner (Illus. 15-1–15-7) being manufactured by the folks who brought us the original PrinceCraft. Although its distribution in the United States is at this time uncertain, it may begin soon. The new joiner has a Börg label. This machine is one of the heaviest of the marketed joiners. Its cord, like that of its predecessor, is very light. Nearly all of the other joiners have rubber cord sets which are $^{21}/_{64}$ inch thick. The Börg joiner has a $^{16}/_{64}$-inch-thick plastic cord. Also, this unit's cord set is very short, just over 5 feet. If this were to be the joiner in my shop, I'd be seriously interested in replacing the entire cord set.

To expose the blade and body on this joiner, simply remove two knurled nuts. This is easier to do on this joiner than on other

Illus. 15-1. Side view of the new Börg/PrinceCraft joiner.

Illus. 15-2. The Börg/PrinceCraft joiner is quite easy to disassemble.

Illus. 15-3. Another disassembled view of the Börg machine.

Illus. 15-4. Disassembled, the tool reveals a very effective blade.

Illus. 15-5–15-7. Three views of the Börg joiner housing.

Illus. 15-6.

Illus. 15-7.

joiners with the exception of the Makita and Lamello Top-Ten joiners.

There are two scales on the front of the Börg's fence. They each have imperial measurements on one side and metric measurements on the other side, rather than a pair of combination scales which might help to ensure a more accurate setup. However, the matching scale would be irrevelant, because the machine also has an accurate single scale on the user side of the fence.

On the side of the machine is a line that marks the top of the blade rather than its center. This line would prove more helpful if it were moved down $5/64$ inch.

The Börg push pins can be adjusted in and out from the outside of the tool. This really seems like an outdated luxury item. Back in the mid- to late '80s, these push pins would have been helpful, but now we prefer the rubber push pads like those on the Freud, Lamello, Sears, and Makita models.

The Börg joiner's six-position depth-of-cut scale has a positive feel without being too tight. Similarly, detents mark the important angles on the flap scale. Unlike the flap faces on the other joiners, the Börg joiner's flap face can be tilted past 90 degrees. However, the Börg joiner does not have an auxiliary fence like that on the Freud or Makita models. This seriously compromises the mitring feature on the machine for those who believe, as I do, that mitres should be cut against the outside rather than the inside of the joint.

Unlike nearly all the other joiners, the Börg has a pair of tie-down holes on either side for bench mounting (Illus. 15-8). The only other machine on which I've seen these is the DeWalt joiner, and on the DeWalt they do not protrude from the side. Also, the dust pickup on the Börg joiner is being improved as I write. If the present pickup is used, the machine will clog.

The Börg joiner may have features that are not required, but which no other machine offers. For example, it can be locked to depth for slotting, grooving, or rabbeting. This machine would be better than most sold for use in North America for cutting the shadow joints that are so commonly used in European panelled ceilings.

The Börg machine is very loud. I measured it at 94 decibels with a Radio Shack Sound Level Meter from 30 inches, which is likely the farthest the tool will ever be from the user's ears. For comparison purposes, it should be noted that the Freud joiner

Illus. 15-8. Top view of the Börg joiner that shows the mounting holes.

measures at 93 decibels, the Makita joiner at 92 decibels, and the Lamello Top-Ten at 91 decibels. If you are making more than a couple of cuts, it's imperative to wear hearing protection of some kind with any of these machines.

The Börg joiner has a powerful cutter, although it has a tendency to "walk" to the left a bit (which is the main reason why I'd really rather see rubber bumpers than push pins for stabilizing); this "walking" isn't necessarily a problem unless you're joining very narrow stock. And on very narrow stock, the Börg joiner will perform better than most of the other joiners.

Below is a chart that compares five critical measurements of Börg, Freud, Makita, and Lamello-Ten joiners.

Dimensions	Lamello Top-Ten	Makita	Freud	Börg
Hand Room	4⅜″	6½″	6″	5⅝″*
Diameter	2⅜″	2⁵⁄₁₆″	2⅜″	2¼″
Blade-Housing Length	7¾″ With Dust Chute 6⅛″ Without Dust Chute	6¾″ With Dust Chute	5⅛″	6″
Height of Fence	3⅜″	3⁹⁄₁₆″	4⁵⁄₁₆″	5³⁄₁₆″
Width of Joiner	5⁹⁄₁₆″ With Knob 4¹⁵⁄₁₆″ Without Knob	5½″	7¼″	6¼″

*Note that the screw for fixing the depth of cut can take up two inches of this space; I'd recommend using the tool without it in place most of the time.

16
Virutex Joiners

In this chapter, two Virutex joiners are described: the O-81 and the AB 11. The O-81 has been discontinued, and replaced by the AB 11. Though the O-81 has been discontinued, there are many used ones available, so the information presented here will prove useful to some woodworkers.

Virutex O-81 Joiner

The Spanish-made Virutex O-81, shown in Illus. 16-1 and 16-2, is imported by Holz Machinery/Rudolf Bass, Inc. Its 500-watt motor produces 10,000 RPM. It weighs seven pounds and has a 7-foot,

Illus. 16-1 (left). A top-down view of the Virutex O-81 joiner. Though this joiner has been discontinued, information is presented in this chapter because there are many used ones available. **Illus. 16-2 (above).** A side view of the Virutex O-81 joiner.

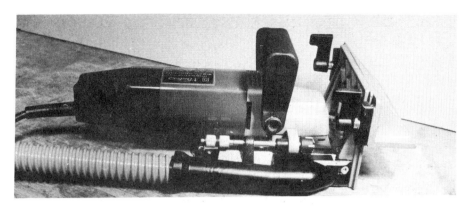

3-inch cord. From two feet away, its noise readings are 101 dB with no load and 104 dB loaded. A dust collector, shown in Illus. 16-3, is available as an option. Its full-year warranty appears to be the industry standard.

The Virutex's manual, while far from comprehensive, is arguably the best of the manuals that accompany the lower-priced machines; this is another factor that should help the tool find its way into more and more amateur shops.

The switch on the Virutex joiner is superior to that on the Freud model because it is easier to operate and is well isolated from

Illus. 16-4. A front view of the Virutex O-81 joiner reveals the inch and milli-metre scales on each side of the faceplate. This is a great aid when you are setting up the cutting gauge and other attachments.

the user under a dustproof, "shock-proof" rubber gasket. There is also a disadvantage to using the switch: It is rather awkwardly placed on the top near the rear of the machine. One cannot assume the correct stance for operating the joiner and then turn it on. It remains to be seen as to whether the position of the switch will lead to any more problems.

The castings of the faceplates and other parts of this machine are of heavier-gauge aluminum and have more ribbing and more accurate layout lines than the castings on the Freud and the other less-expensive models. The faceplate on the Virutex is ruled in both inches and millimetres on each side of the casting (Illus. 16-4). Another desirable feature is its quick-adjust depth-of-cut scale that permits the user to select number 0, 10, or 20 biscuits in virtually no time at all and switch easily from size to size.

Though the Virutex joiner seems longer than the other joiners, it isn't; however, there is no chance of pinching your fingers while operating it. Indeed, it is one of the most comfortable joiners to operate, and it becomes even more comfortable with its optional dust-collection hose in place. A vacuum-assisted dust-collection system is more of a necessity than optional, especially if you use the tool left-handed.

The fence adjusters are accurate and square, but you can't turn the large lock-down knobs, shown in Illus. 16-5, through a full 360 degrees without hitting the rear supports of the faceplate.

Illus. 16-5. The large tabs that control the tightness of the Virutex 0-81 joiner's fixed-angle fence sometimes hit the bracket that mounts the faceplate to the joiner's base.

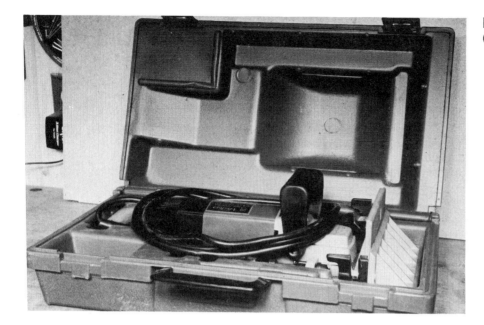

When the screw that holds the tightening knob in place fell off one side of a Virutex I was using, I discovered that it was easier to adjust the machine, and became convinced that I could use the machine for a long time without replacing that screw. If the machine had been my own, I would have promptly removed the other side's mating screw.

The Virutex is one of two machines whose case doesn't strain the "relief" portion of the cord. (The "relief" portion to the cord is the first 4–6 inches of the cord as it comes out of the body of the tool. This portion is quite a bit thicker than the rest of the cord, and provides a "strain relief" against the possibility of the cord being twisted until it breaks or is pulled out of the tool.) Furthermore, the "used" Virutex I sampled demonstrated the longevity of these injection-moulded cases; the case, as shown in Illus. 16-6, appears to have been used a great deal, yet it remains serviceable. Though it shows signs of wear, it shows no signs of deterioration.

Virutex AB 11 Joiner

The Virutex AB 11 joiner replaces the now discontinued O-81 joiner. It is made of finer heavy-grade aluminum (Illus. 16-7). Its 10,000 RPM motor, at 550 watts, has more power than the motor

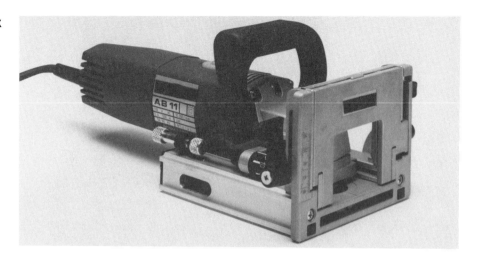

Illus. 16-7. The Virutex AB 11 joiner.

on the O-81. And the machine is markedly more quiet. In fact, although the O-81 joiner was a reliable machine that will prove a good bargain in the used-tool market, the Virutex AB 11 is vastly superior to it.

The Virutex AB 11 joiner comes with a standard dust pickup adapter that is very easy to use. The adapter simply slides into a channel on the side of the joiner. It can be screwed into place, but this might be required only if the machine will see a great deal of use with the dust pickup attached. On the other hand, I screwed the dust pickup onto my machine as soon as I got it into my shop.

Like most other biscuit joiners, the AB 11 comes with a case (Illus. 16-8). Its case is made of injected plastic, so it is very much a form-fit. One disadvantage is that you can't use both the case and

Illus. 16-8. The Virutex AB 11 joiner in its fitted case.

Illus. 16-9 (above left). Biscuiting a mitre in composition material. Making the mitre this way aligns the insides of the material. **Illus. 16-10 (above right).** Making a divider joint with the Virutex AB 11.

the dust pickup, because the case isn't form-fit for use with that attachment. Perhaps the function of these cases is to prevent damage to the tool when it is shipped overseas and/or across country. If the machine were mine to keep, I'd throw the case away!

If you were to look at the machine from the front, you would note that the knob on the right of the machine adjusts the flap face. These large, easy-to-adjust knobs should be a standard for the industry. The height of the flap adjusts from the left. The faceplate is scaled in both inches and millimetres. Rubber bumpers have replaced the push pins of the earlier model. I've used both systems enough to know that the rubber system holds the workpiece in place at least as well as the prongs, and it is less likely to mar the work. The switch has a safety lock.

The fence and flap-face features are as complicated and have to be adjusted as much as those on any joiner. A contractor friend found these complicated systems to be less than absolutely reliable unless they are set up with extreme care. This system is made of castings rather than sheet metal, and it appears to be composed of very tight, square fits, so it may be less likely than some of the others to work its way out of square over time.

17
Lamello Joiners

The original edition of *Biscuit Joiner Handbook* contained information on the Lamello Top, the Lamello Junior, and the Lamello Standard. These joiners have been discontinued. The Lamello Top-Ten has replaced the Top, and the Standard-Ten and Cobra have replaced the Junior and Standard machines. The Top-Ten, the Standard-Ten, and the Cobra are discussed in this chapter.

Top-Ten

The Swiss-made Lamello Top-Ten, which has superseded the Top, is almost certain to appear at or near the top of everyone's list of desirable joiners (Illus. 17-1–17-3). The name Top-Ten is a reference to ten features on the joiner that are an improvement on the original Top's features.

Illus. 17-1. The Lamello Top-Ten (left) has superseded the Lamello Top.

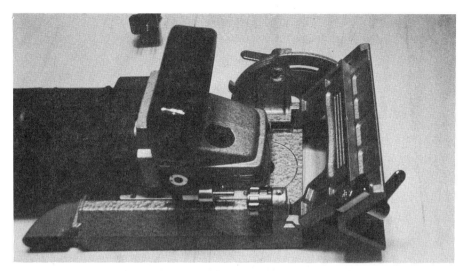

Illus. 17-2. Side view of the Top-Ten set up to cut mitres from the outside of the joint.

Illus. 17-3. The Lamello Top-Ten in its case.

Smoother and more convenient than the Top, the Top-Ten is perhaps the fastest and easiest joiner to use that's available today, and arguably the best balanced. There is also less vibration transferred to the operator's hands. Its 700-watt, 10,000-RPM motor cuts without hesitation in even the toughest material.

The machine weighs seven pounds and has a cord that's 8 feet, 6 inches long. Its wooden case is much larger than that of its predecessor—one no longer has to worry about damaging the "strain relief" cord—and it has a very convenient accessory storage space.

The sound level of the joiner is 93 dB loaded or unloaded. The machine comes from the factory with a pair of dust outlets, one of which can be attached to a piece of vacuum cleaner hose of your choice rather than the expensive attachment that was supplied with the Top.

The joiner has a flap-front faceplate with an accurate protractor added to it. Its fixed-angle attachment has sliding dovetails for quick and accurate attachment to, and removal from, the faceplate. There is now a height scale that can be read through the back of the attachment when it is used (Illus. 17-4 and 17-5). The joiner's adjustable head doesn't require us to make jigs and supports for joining angles other than 90 or 45 degrees.

The Top-Ten retains the 4-millimetre attachment plate that permits the joiner to center on both three-quarter and half-inch material; this plastic plate changes the position of the blade relative to the flap-front faceplate. The plate also helps speed the spacing of multiple-width biscuit joints in thick material.

The powerful motor on the Lamello Top-Ten is slip-clutch-protected, and its switch is the easiest one to use (though I still prefer the switch on the Elu joiner). It has a spindle lock that makes blade changing markedly easy, and an easy-off bottom for blade changing or for changing dust-ejection chutes. It has a pair of anti-slip pads instead of the spring-loaded positioning pins. They are just as effective.

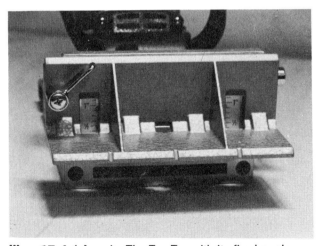

Illus. 17-4 (above). The Top-Ten with its fixed-angle attachment showing read-through scales. **Illus. 17-5 (right).** The Top-Ten with its flap-front faceplate.

The Top-Ten has six depths of cut on its depth scale: 0, 10, 20, max, D, and S (Illus. 17-6). The first three represent the stock Lamello biscuit sizes. Max indicates maximum depth of cut, S the depth for Simplex connectors, and D the proper depths for Lamello Paumelle hinges.

The least-desirable aspect of the Lamello Top-Ten joiner is its high list price. However, it is such a well-made machine that if you could afford the luxury of the added expense, perhaps you should consider buying it.

Any accessories Lamello offers can be used with the Top-Ten. These accessories are discussed in depth in Chapter 25.

Standard-Ten and Cobra Joiners

Lamello has replaced its Junior and Standard machines with the Standard-Ten (Illus. 17-7). The Standard-Ten is the ideal machine to set up with the numerous Lamello accessories.

The Lamello is also marketing another joiner, the Cobra. The Cobra runs at 250 watts and 15,000 RPM, and is 5.5 pounds. It uses a massive two-tooth carbide cutter which is almost as large as a shaper cutter.

Like all Lamello joiners, the Cobra comes in a well-organized

Illus. 17-6. A close-up view of the depth-of-cut mechanism on the Lamello Top-Ten.

Illus. 17-7. Comparing the Lamello Standard-Ten (right) with the Lamello Top-Ten (left). The main difference is the flap faceplate.

case (Illus. 17-8). It is also much more comfortable to hold than most other joiners (Illus. 17-9). Like the other Lamello models, its right-angle head attaches squarely to the faceplate. It has an angle stub for cutting mitres that is very handy (Illus. 17-10).

I used a Lamello Cobra in an area where the ambient noise was 77–78 dB. The Cobra raised the level to 95 dB when measured from 30 inches—the distance from the tool to my ears.

One possible drawback is that it takes a few seconds for the trigger-operated motor on the Cobra to sound as if it has reached full speed, and it takes at least a second and a half from switch-on to first plunge. There is no way to lock the power on. While this might be a problem in the professional shop, where time means money, it shouldn't pose a problem in the hobby shop.

The parts kit for a Cobra includes 1 hinge, 1 C20 biscuit, 1 K20 biscuit, 1 pair of K-D biscuits, and 8 generic biscuits (two each of four sizes). Also included is a spring remover, oil, a Phillips head

Illus. 17-8. The Lamello Cobra with its case and accessories.

Illus. 17-9. A close-up of the Lamello Cobra.

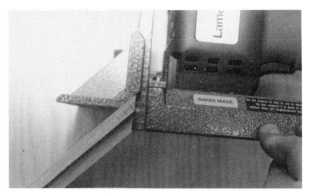

Illus. 17-10. Cutting 45-degree angles with the Cobra is easier than with other joiners because the Cobra has a notch in its faceplate.

screwdriver, a pair of spanners for changing the blade, an extra pair of anti-slip pads, and an instruction manual. In short, the Cobra offers the hobbyist woodworker a complete introduction to the Lamello system at a reasonable price.

Responding to an article in *Better Homes & Gardens Wood* magazine, which suggested that a basic feature for all "quality" biscuit joiners is a swivel faceplate, Lamello will eventually introduce a Cobra-Ten and a Standard-Ten-A with swivel faceplates. The Cobra and Standard-Ten that are available now will remain available.

18
DeWalt DW682 Plate Joiner

The DeWalt DW682 plate joiner, built and distributed by Black & Decker, is made in the United States. Tool distributors I have spoken with suggest that this joiner would prove to be very popular. Black & Decker must be convinced of the tool's quality, because it offers a 30-day money-back guarantee, the only such guarantee in the industry. It is also sold under the Elu name.

The DeWalt joiner is smallish and lightweight. Its motor runs at 6.5 amps and at 10,000 RPM. Its ⅛-inch sheet stock base plate will prove very helpful when you have to clamp the tool to a variety of shop-made jigs (Illus. 18-1). Its fingertip switch on the underside

Illus. 18-1. This view of the underside of the DeWalt joiner shows a flat, clean surface with easy-to-use markings. The bottom of this joiner makes it easy to use on jigs and fixtures.

of the grinder body is unlike that on any other joiner, working more like a trigger than a switch. The dust bag and dust-chute connection are both standard (Illus. 18-2). Certainly, there's little excuse for not using one or the other when biscuit-joining.

This joiner, like the Porter-Cable joiner, registers for mitre cuts against the outside of the workpiece. It also has a rack-and-pinion mechanism that keeps the up-down adjustment both square and precise and a moving flap face (Illus. 18-3).

Illus. 18-2. Everything comes standard with the DeWalt joiner, even the dust pickup kit.

Illus. 18-3. The flap face rides up and down the fixed face on a rack-and-pinion mechanism to ensure that it remains square.

I had to add a pair of number 10 washers to make the movable faceplate lock down properly. The machine's faceplate appeared too loose to use, but I couldn't confirm through Black & Decker whether this is a problem common to all machines or just to my sample. In any event, my solution was simple, very inexpensive, and absolutely foolproof.

The manual clips into the lid of the tool box (Illus. 18-4). If Black & Decker is generous, it will release its patent rights on this feature so other manufacturers might follow suit. The DeWalt tool box is very well designed.

At 94 dB, the DeWalt joiner would qualify as "average" among joiners in noise level. This reading—94dB—would have qualified the DeWalt joiner as very quiet several years ago. While the DeWalt joiner may rate as "average" in terms of noise, I would rate it as one of the two or three best joiners in terms of overall use.

Illus. 18-4. The DeWalt case is unusual in that it has a spring in its lid that holds the manual in place.

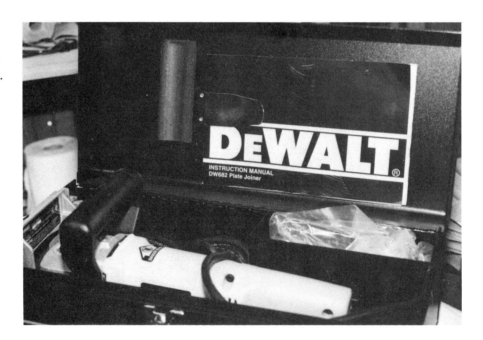

19

Stationary Biscuit Joiners

Until recently, the biscuit joiners available to American wood-workers were all portable. Even if you already have a portable joiner in your cabinet shop, you are sure to appreciate the convenience of the joiners discussed here: the Delta 32-100 and the Norfield Jointmaster.

Delta 32-100 Joiner

The Delta joiner was the first stationary joiner available in this country (Illus. 19-1 and 19-2). This 40-pound unit, which is meant to be fastened to a bench, offers more features than the portable tools. For example, it has an 8 × 12-inch adjustable table that rides through five inches of adjustment against a finely machined face. Its 10-amp motor drives a standard 10,000 RPM 4-inch slotting cutter via a Super-Torque belt. The cutterhead moves into the work when the operator steps on a cable-operated foot switch. A spring returns the cutter to the ready position without inducing the back-lash one might reasonably expect. This joiner, which runs at a noise level of 89–90 dB, is quieter than any of the portables on the market.

The Delta 32-100 joiner is convenient to use. There are quick-release threads on the height adjustment and hold-down screws. A fine-adjusting knob makes precise work positioning possible and quick. These components ensure accuracy. The hold-down clamp is so easy to use that woodworkers actually use it! The 8 × 12-inch adjustable table and the face on which it rides have both been machined to accept the clamp's tight-fitting square base; thus, it is possible to clamp both horizontal and vertical work. For some angle cutting, you may have to use another clamp to hold the work firmly on the cutting table. Additionally, when cutting bevels, it is good practice to clamp a backup stop block to the angle fence to take the place of Delta's adjustable stop stock on the regular table.

The angle guide on older models, such as the one shown in Illus. 19-1 and 19-2, is a steel tilting table provided for joining angled work. (Newer Delta joiners do not have the auxiliary tilting table. Instead, their redesigned standard table now tilts 45 degrees upwards for bevel-joining jobs.) This is far handier than the guides on most of the other joiners, and is extremely accurate. Note that the levers that lock the tilting table in place are spring-loaded, so they can easily be positioned out of the way. As with the portable joiners, the best practice is to bevel both pieces of an angled joint at the same angle. If, for some reason, they aren't, the biscuit slots must be cut at the same angle anyway, because the biscuits can't be "flexed" to fit.

 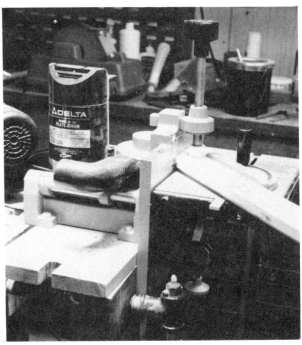

Illus. 19-1 (above left). Front view of the Delta 32-100 mounted to my workbench. **Illus. 19-2 (above right).** Side view of the Delta 32-100 mounted to my workbench.

One has to pay more attention to the angle fences when using stationary joiners. Even with the Delta 32-100, it is possible to mitre *through* the stock, ruining it and harming both the blade and the mitre table. It may be worth noting that most portable biscuit joiners work best at 45 or 90 degrees, but the 32-100, like the Lamello Top-Ten, will cut handily at any angle.

What looks like the tool's mitre gauge is actually an adjustable stock stop which can be positioned anywhere on the table with either right- or left-hand reference, and then screwed into place from the underside of the table. If you will be adjusting this regularly, then you will not want to leave the angle guide hanging under the main worktable, as the owner's manual recommends.

Layout is even easier with this machine than with a standard biscuit joiner, especially if you have repeated cuts. Just mark out the first piece, clamp the board and the guide, and make the cut. After the first cut is made, just clamp the next board in place. If the boards being joined are not the same thickness, they must be positioned on the joiner "good"-sides down.

Since the face on the Delta 32-100 indicates the exact width of cut *and* the centerline, the layout lines on the face are slightly less than the minimum width. Actually, a board that fits close to the size-20 layout lines should probably be joined with a size-10 biscuit to ensure a trouble-free joint. Edge-to-edge joining, like most joining, is the same with this machine as with any of the hand-held models, except that with all but the largest boards, it is easier to bring the material to the joiner rather than vice versa. This is the real advantage of this stationary machine.

It does not appear likely that butt joints more than 5 inches from either end of a board or panel can be made with this machine. Since most buyers will already have hand-held joiners, this inability shouldn't outweigh the 32-100's many other advantages.

Because my shop is chronically short of space, I have mounted the Delta 32-100 on a 1 × 8¾ × 20-inch board, so that I can clamp it to my bench quickly when I need it. The *ideal* base would be about 8 inches lower, so the work height would be closer to that of the bench or a table saw. Now that the tool has been in my shop for a couple of years, I am firmly convinced that it has been underrated on nearly all counts. Though you still can't cut internal T joints with it, for all other standard biscuit operations the Delta is fast and accurate. This is one of the best bargains available.

Norfield Jointmaster

The Norfield Jointmaster is an expensive, professional stationary biscuit joiner with many precision features (Illus. 19-3 and 19-4). Precision fences and adjustable stops allow repeatable accuracy with very little setup time, regardless of operator expertise. A foot pedal frees both hands, permitting fast, easy control of material. There are quick-change devices for moving from face to edge cuts, and quick-change depth-of-cut settings. Pneumatic clamps provide precise material location and improved operator safety; these clamps are so quick and foolproof that you will use them automatically.

This tool has more capabilities than any amateur "home" user is likely to need. Indeed, the minimal manual seems to be geared to professional users. Nevertheless, more than a single page of typed instructions concerning cutting techniques, blade removal, etc., might help purchasers to better protect their fairly considerable investment. Since the tool's main advantage is speed, I'm somewhat disconcerted by the amount of experimentation that precision adjustment will likely take. The unit *is* indeed nearly perfect as it comes from the factory, but keeping it this way is sure to take some effort.

Illus. 19-3 (above left). The Norfield Jointmaster. **Illus. 19-4 (above right).** Close-up of the Norfield Jointmaster.

The 75-pound tool sits on an all-steel stand that is 30 inches high by 18 inches deep. This stand puts the work at a comfortable height of 41¾ inches. An 8 × 20-inch table supports all but the largest work handily. A 5⅝ × 20-inch-square back complements the table for nearly all square work. Also included as standard equipment is a sturdy, precision-aligned 8 × 18-inch, 45-degree mitre fence which references the outside of the joint. A 22½-degree mitre fence is an optional accessory. One advantage of these fences is that they have been registered so that they can't be installed out of square. Stainless-steel stop tubes extend the effective working length of the machine from 20 to 66 inches; three stops are provided for each side, although longer tubes and extra stops are available options. The stops are particularly convenient, for their spring-loaded fingers slide easily out of the way when it's necessary to cut past a stop; no longer is it absolutely necessary to work from longest to shortest stops. The stop system is great for work in production settings because it eliminates the need for constant or repetitive layout. Rounding out these convenience features is a standard 1½-inch chip-evacuation chute to which a Shop-Vac or other dust-collection system can be readily attached.

The totally enclosed ⅓-horsepower motor powers a direct-drive 4-inch-diameter, 12-tooth blade which can be adjusted from ⅛ to 1½ inches above the table. Eighty to 100 PSI of air (at less than 1 CFM) is required for operation. The air operates three main controls: the plunge-cut control, the blade-retract control, and the clamp-release control. The plunge-cut control adjusts the speed at which the blade enters the wood. The blade-retract control can be set considerably faster than the plunge-cut control, for it merely removes the blade from the wood. The clamp-release control must be adjusted to ensure that it always releases the wood after the blade retracts.

Sooner or later comparisons are sure to be made between the Norfield and the only other stationary joiner readily available, the Delta 32-100. At 1⅜ inches, the vertical blade-travel range of the Norfield joiner is less than the Delta's. This does not particularly matter, because biscuit-joining internal members is a job that can be done only with hand-held joiners. The Jointmaster's table is nearly twice the size of the Delta table, and, at 75 pounds, the tool is markedly less "portable." My Delta joiner rests on a shelf. When I need a stationary biscuit joiner, getting it out takes only slightly longer than attaching the air hose to the Jointmaster, which also takes up valuable shop space when it's not being used.

The most overwhelming difference between the two joiners is that the Delta joiner does not have the stop system, air clamps, and many of the other sophisticated features of the Norfield Jointmaster. The Jointmaster is considerably more expensive than the Delta joiner, and it is reasonable to expect it to have more sophisticated features. Obviously, the Norfield Jointmaster is only for the most affluent craftspeople, yet in production settings, where time is

Feature	Delta 32-100	Norfield Jointmaster
Address	Delta International Machinery Corp. 246 Alpha Drive Pittsburgh, PA 15238	Norfield Industries 3760 Morrow Lane, Suite E Chico, CA 95928
Country of origin	Taiwan	United States
List price	$329 (widely discounted)	$499 (firm)
Cutters	Twelve 4″ T carbide cutters	Twelve 4″ T carbide (Elu) cutters
Vertical blade travel	5″	$1\frac{3}{8}$″
Weight	40 pounds	75 pounds
Motor specifications	10 amp (Taiwanese)	5 amps ($\frac{1}{3}$ HP TEFC Dayton)
Table size	8 × 12	8 × 20
Angle-joining capabilities	All angles	90°, 45°, optional $22\frac{1}{2}$°
Base	None	30″ high
Clamping	2 positions	2 positions (air-powered)
Material to be cut	Hard and soft woods, sheet stock	Soft woods, sheet stock
Additional features		Adjustable stops

Table 19-1. A comparison of the features on the Delta 32-100 joiner and the Norfield Jointmaster.

valuable and good help is not available, you're sure to get more superior results with the Jointmaster than I achieved in my own shop. If you require superior results, use lots of biscuits, and if efficiency is essential, this joiner will prove to be a worthwhile investment.

ShopSmith Attachment

ShopSmith owners will be pleased to note that there is a biscuit-joining attachment designed for use on the ShopSmith Mark V (Illus. 19-5 and 19-6) and for use on your drill press (Illus. 19-7). This attachment is easy to set up and will provide strong, accurate joints that can be quickly made. *Popular Science* magazine called this product "one of the top 100 products of the year" in 1988.

Illus. 19-5. The Shop-Smith biscuit joiner accessory. Also see Illus. 19-6 and 19-7 on the following page.

Illus. 19-6. The Shop-Smith biscuit joiner in use on a ShopSmith machine.

Illus. 19-7. The Shop-Smith biscuit joiner mounted to a five-speed drill press. Always use a dust-collection system. This is a quicker and easier method of collecting the dust than sweeping it.

20
Sears Biscuit Joiners and Accessories

Bis-Kit

The Bis-Kit accessory will permit you to sample biscuit joinery without having to spend money on a a professional joiner. It is designed to fit on almost any router with a 6-inch round base, which includes all recent Craftsman routers as well as many others (Illus. 20-1–20-4). Additionally, one could probably redrill the Bis-Kit's platform to fit virtually any other router. However, there's little reason to do this when there's an inexpensive router as good as the Sears 17471 to attach to it. This router features micro-depth adjust-

Illus. 20-1 and 20-2. Two views of the Bis-Kit mounted to a router. It is being used to sand on the router's top. The router's flat top makes it easier to attach accessories to it.

Illus. 20-3. The Bis-Kit with its component groups. On the right is the Bis-Kit jig and its cutter. On the left is the router, which must be purchased separately.

Illus. 20-4. The Bis-Kit as the operator would most likely pick it up from the bench.

ment and a scale graduated in ⅟₆₄-inch increments across its 0–1½ inches range. The cam-lever locking is easy to operate. The 17471's flat top with built-in wrench storage makes mounting accessories like the Bis-Kit very easy.

Ten minutes of assembly yields a mostly plastic, but very sturdy accessory router base that will effectively permit one to make biscuited edge joints with a router. After this initial assembly, one can attach it to a router in well under five minutes. It is a good idea to mount the cutter to the router's collet before mounting the Bis-Kit assembly.

As Illus. 20-5 shows, the three-tooth, carbide-tipped wing cutter can enter the work only on or very near its edges. All vertical adjustments are done with the router's depth-of-cut gauge, and the horizontal adjustments with the Bis-Kit depth-of-cut gauge. As usual, Sears' manual is a model of clarity.

Test cuts show that the unit performs exactly as specified. If the fairly long setup times don't bother you, if you already have a router and expect to do little biscuit joining, buy this very inexpensive attachment. However, if you have to buy the router and the Bis-Kit at the same time, buying an inexpensive joiner might make more sense. Routers are invariably somewhat louder than are grinder-based biscuit joiners, and only the occasional hobbyist woodworker can afford the setup time that an accessory like this requires. On the other hand, another router could prove helpful in the workshop, and a relatively inexpensive router like the Craftsman 17471 has enough features to be desirable for far more than running the Bis-Kit jig.

The Bis-Kit differs from grinder-based joiners in basically only two ways. First, the layouts have to be marked about 3¼ inches long, so they are visible all through the cutting. Second, besides being plunged into the work, the tool must be slid along the work for nearly an inch to get the desired length of cut. Hobbyist woodworkers should find these differences inconsequential. In the important respects, this tool is much like the commercial joiners. It makes edge-to-edge joints, corner joints, and butt joints that can be readily assembled with water-based glue that causes the biscuits to grow.

Like some other manufacturers' stationary biscuit joiners,

Illus. 20-5. The Bis-Kit's cutter.

which are all at least several times more expensive, there's one cut the Bis-Kit won't make: a T-joint cut. This is a cut that is very seldom made. If you do make a lot of these cuts, you're probably already a candidate for the best angle-grinder-based biscuit joiner your local Sears store can provide.

The Bis-Kit's 2-inch carbide blade cuts all woods; the depth of cut is adjustable to the three sizes of biscuits via an adjustment on the jig, and up and down via the router's depth-of-cut adjustment.

The Bis-Kit is best for joining edges. The biscuits provide strong, invisible joints for a variety of glued-up panels and also for picture frames that are at least 23⅛ inches wide across the 45-degree diagonal.

As you experiment with biscuit joinery, you're sure to find plenty of uses for this accessory. Ed Veome, Craftsman's biscuit joiner expert, says, "It's fast and easy to make accurate, professional-looking joints in less time with no hassles." Since 1989, this tool has given thousands of woodworking hobbyists a taste of biscuit joinery. This taste is all many of us will ever need.

Illus. 20-6–20-8 show a simple jig that be can be used to turn the Bis-Kit into a simple stationary joiner. Jigs like this are usually

Illus. 20-6. Front view of the Bis-Kit stationary jig. In use, you would have to clamp the feet of the jig to the bench.

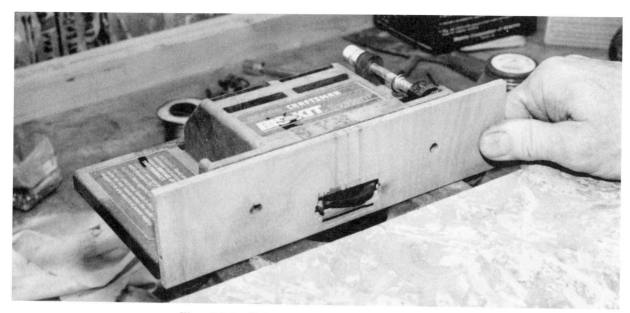

Illus. 20-7. This view of the Bis-Kit stationary jig shows the cutter coming into play as the jig starts to operate.

Illus. 20-8. This back view of the jig shows how the router virtually rides the table.

made of scrap stock, so the dimensions of yours may vary from those of the machine shown in the photographs. That machine is $32 \times 5\frac{1}{2}$ inches, just tall enough to let the router clear it; indeed, as the photographs illustrate, the router all but rests on its "top."

Sears Craftsman #17501 Plate Joiner

Sears' first dedicated plate joiner was designed almost entirely from the user's point of view (Illus. 20-9). The new plate joiner was not drafted from a right-angle grinder, but specifically for the natural motion of joining two pieces of wood using a dedicated power tool (Illus. 20-10).

Illus. 20-9. The Sears Craftsman 17501 plate joiner. (Courtesy of Sears)

Illus. 20-10. The front-assist handle aids in the cutting operation. (Courtesy of Sears)

Specifications of Sears Joiner #17501

Horsepower	$\frac{5}{8}$
Amps	6.0
Voltage	120 volt, 60 HZ AC only
Speeds	10,000 RPM no load
Switch Type	Trigger (actuated micro-switch)
Cord	10′ SJTW-A (moulded bend relief)
Brushes	Nonaccessible
Motor Housing	Clamshell polycarbonate (MT1055-5)
Gear Case	Die-cast zinc
Rear Handle	Contoured, enclosed, pistol grip
Front Handle	Palm
Fence Type	Adjustable
Fence Angles	0–90 degrees
Positive Stops	0, 15, 30, 45, 60, 90 degrees, with highlighted scale (within 1 degree accuracy)
Adj. Fence Height	0–2.0″ with 0–1.5″ scale
Fence Height Scale	$\frac{1}{16}$″ increments
Sight Line Opening	Yes, with line-up mark on both fences & base sides
Fence Material	5% G.F. polycarbonate (MT 1055-5)
Faceplate Material	5% G.F. polycarbonate (MT 1055-5)
Faceplate Backing Pad	Rubber-coated foam
Chip Collection	Yes, with dust box
Depth of Cut	0–$\frac{5}{8}$″ minimum
Micro Depth Adjustment	Yes
Hardware	Knobs
Bearings	Ball/sleeve
Biscuit Sizes Compatible	#0, #10, #20
Pre-Set Depth-of-Cut Adj.	3 positions
Cutter Type	4-inch, 8-tooth carbide-tipped
Drive Type	Single-reduction helical
Color	Black tool & box; charcoal-grey fences
Regulatory Approvals	UL/CSA (North America only)
Grounding	Double-insulated
Owner's Manual	English
Biscuit Assortment	20 biscuits of #10 size
Warranty	1 year

Table 20-1. A description of the features of the Sears Craftsman 17501 plate joiner.

The sloping, contoured rear handle is designed for better comfort and control. Its front fence with depth and bevel scales is adjustable to 2 inches in height and 0 to 90 degrees, for joining bevelled workpieces.

The nonslip vertical fence is designed for positive contact with the work surface to prevent "rocking" or slippage during use. An integrated front-assist handle aids in guiding the plate joiner through the cutting operation.

The ⅝ horsepower, 6-amp motor provides enough power to easily handle most soft and hard woods. The joiner's internal helical gearing provides a smooth transfer of power to the cutter. Its combination no-load speed of 10,000 RPM and 4-inch, 8-tooth blade provides fast, clean cuts.

The Craftsman Plate Joiner also offers a three-position depth-of-cut system with microfine adjustments to accept #0, #10, and #20 biscuits. Other features include a sawdust/chip collection box located in the rear of the tool and a 10-foot cord with cord clip for easy storage.

21
Skil 1605 Biscuit Joiner and the Wolfcraft Multi-Shaper Kit

In this chapter the Skil 1605 biscuit joiner (Illus. 21-1) and the Wolfcraft Multi-Shaper Kit are examined and described. These two products are included together in one chapter because the Skil joiner is basically a Wolfcraft Multi-Shaper Kit mounted on a Skil grinder.

Illus. 21-1. The Skil 1605 joiner.

Skil's affordable new joiner is assembled in the United States. Based on the Skil professional-grade disc grinder, it runs at 5.5 amps and 12,000 RPM. The tool is basically a disc grinder with a permanently mounted conversion kit similar to the one that Wolfcraft has had available for the past couple of years (Illus. 21-2). The Skil biscuit joiner comes in a very large carrying case, which has room in it for more than just the tool (Illus. 21-3). A dust bag is permanently mounted to the tool. This is the type of joiner that the average woodworker will be able to buy off the shelf in his neighbor-

Illus. 21-2. The Skil 1605 joiner is one of the few joiners that comes apart quickly.

Illus. 21-3. The Skil 1605 joiner in its large, useful case.

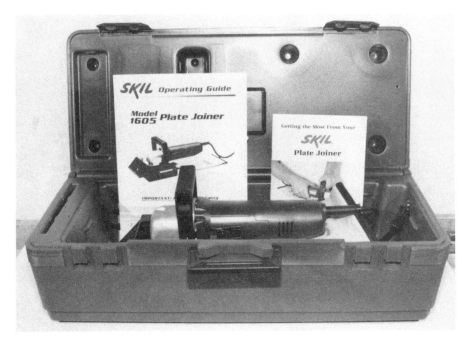

hood home center. The others all appear to be bought through a professional tool dealer or through mail order.

In Europe, the four-inch grinder is used nearly as often as the electric drill. European homeowners, do-it-yourselfers, and craftspeople have far more use for the small grinder than do Americans. In fact, most American woodworkers have never even used one. All this may change because Wolfcraft of America, the United States arm of a major German tooling company, has introduced the Multi-Shaper, a device that performs all the standard biscuit-slotting operations while powered by such a grinder (Illus. 21-4).

The Skil 1605 joiner is modelled after the Multi-Shaper. Both are made of fibre-reinforced acrylic, which gives the joiners rigid strength and makes them inexpensive. Both come with a dust bag. Unlike the Skil joiner, the Multi-Shaper comes with a textless instruction manual that still clarifies how to both assemble your grinder and operate the completed "joiner." If you have a four-inch grinder that's just lying around most of the time, this kit may be just what you need. If you don't have a grinder, you're sure to prefer the Skil joiner.

Illus. 21-4. Front view of the Wolfcraft Multi-Shaper.

There have been several changes to these tools since they were introduced. The depth adjustment now has a dial setting for #0, #10, and #20 biscuits. The ball bearings are of better quality. Rubber feet have been added to prevent the machine from skidding across the work. A vacuum adapter will be added for dust collection. Most notably, an accessory flap-front fence will become available. Thus, these inexpensive joiners are sure to be popular with many woodworkers.

22
Ryobi JM-100 Biscuit Joiner

The Ryobi JM-100 is the first Japanese joiner to reach the American market (Illus. 22-1 and 22-2). Running at 5.3 amps and 9,000 RPM, the Ryobi joiner is a quality tool offered at an economical price. Its 4-inch-diameter blade runs on a ⅞-inch spindle, the

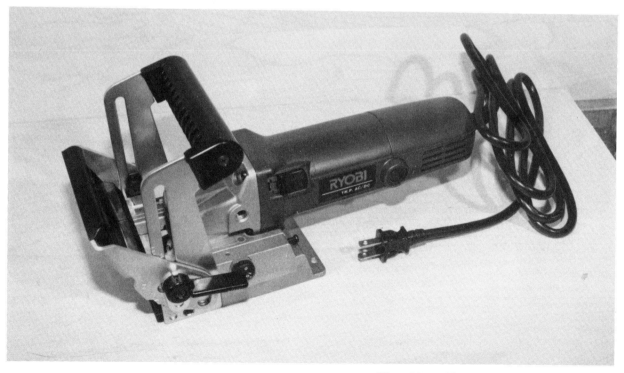

Illus. 22-1. The Ryobi JM-100 biscuit joiner.

Illus. 22-2. The Ryobi JM-100 joiner in its excellent metal case.

largest in the industry. It will cut as deep as $^{25}\!/_{32}$ inches, but it adjusts readily to the #0, #10, and #20 biscuit sizes. Its large fence adjusts from 0 to 180 degrees, so it can be used to cut mitres against either the inside or the outside of the workpiece (Illus. 22-3 and 22-4). Most joiners would require a series of blocks to do this. The faceplate has been completely covered with rubber to make it absolutely steady. The machine comes with a standard dust bag.

Illus. 22-3. The Ryobi JM-100 joiner set up for 45-degree mitring. Note that this setup permits the outsides of the mitres to meet.

Illus. 22-4. The unique design of the Ryobi JM-100 faceplate permits it to be used at many different angles.

Offering the largest faceplate and fence of any of the joiners, the Ryobi has a 2¼-inch straight slotting capacity, compared to a 1½-inch capacity for the Lamello Top-Ten and most other joiners (Illus. 22-5 and 22-6). It is 11⁷⁄₁₆ inches long by 6¹¹⁄₃₂ inches wide by 6 inches high.

The D-handle on the Ryobi joiner is straight and square to the rest of the joiner. Most other D-handles are so awkward to use that far too many joiner users ignore this important safety feature. In fact, left-handers can turn the D-handle on the Ryobi joiner around, and find it comfortable to use.

Illus. 22-5. The Ryobi JM-100 joiner set up for "normal" square joining.

Illus. 22-6. The Ryobi JM-100 joiner will often be used in this "straight" setting.

The Ryobi joiner is used the same as the Porter-Cable joiner when it comes to mitring carcass corners in materials less than 1½ inches thick. In thicker stock, set the fence at 135 degrees and mitre as you would with every other joiner. No other joiner offers this feature.

The JM-100 is one of the quietest joiners on the market, a feature worth considering if you will be using the tool for hours at a time. The motor brushes are replaceable. The tool's lock-on switch is in perfect position for the thumb of a right-handed user, but left-handed users will have to put a dust bag or pickup hose in place.

Since I last used the tool, two important modifications have been made to the machine. First, the dust-bag exhaust port design has been changed so that the bag comes off at a 7-degree angle rather than parallel to the motor. This enhances the user's ability to hold the machine closer to the head, which will improve accuracy and comfort while using it. Perhaps even more important, the fence footprint has been modified. The old fence system, shown in the illustrations in this chapter, left a rather large gap between the fence and the housing. This could cause difficulty during tricky vertical end cuts on very narrow pieces of material. The modification to the fence ensures that more of the material touches the housing of the tool. This enhances the tool's capabilities.

23
Bosch B1650 Biscuit Joiner

The Bosch B1650 joiner is available from a company long known for its extremely high-quality tools. The tool requires 700 watts at 5.8 amps to produce a no-load speed of 11,000 RPM. Standard equipment includes a dust bag, a blade, a case, a very serviceable glue bottle, and 20 biscuits (10 of size #20, and 5 each of sizes #0 and #10). Only the Bosch AirSweep dust hose is optional. The tool is assembled in the United States.

When I first opened the case, I was pleased to see the standard dust bag and glue bottle (Illus. 23-1). Isn't it about time that

Illus. 23-1. The Bosch B1650 joiner in its fitted case. Note the standard glue bottle.

someone started including a dust *bottle* as standard equipment? The dust-bag connector is a perfect fit for the Bosch AirSweep system (Illus. 23-2 and 23-3), and I highly recommend that you use the Bosch AirSweep System.

The cord set is of typical Bosch quality. The switch (Illus. 23-4) is well positioned for right-handed users, and not as awkward for left-handers as most. The operating handle (Illus. 23-5) is more comfortable than the standard D-handle found on most joiners, and makes the tool comfortable to use with either hand. All the knobs are comfortable to use.

The joiner body is made of fibreglass-reinforced plastic. This may perfectly suit the extremely inexpensive joiners, but a high-quality material should be used on this version, which is more expensive. I have broken tools and fixtures made with this material, although this did not happen with the Bosch joiner.

The Bosch B1650 joiner, a moderately priced tool, is competing with established machines which have more features. For starters, it offers only the #0, #10, and #20 biscuit positions (Illus. 23-6) rather than the six positions of the top-line joiners. The awkward rear depth-of-cut setting and the difficult-to-see depth-of-cut indicator are reminiscent of the Skil joiner or the WolfCraft

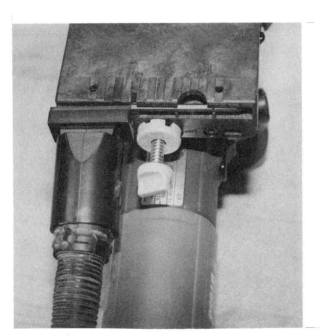 

Illus. 23-2 and 23-3. The dust-bag holder also holds the Bosch AirSweep dust pickup base.

attachment for your own grinder motor. Lest this portion of the review sound completely negative, it should be noted that this set-up system makes fine adjustment for precise fits for the three standard sizes of biscuits far easier than it is on most joiners. Negating this advantage, however, is the manufacturer's suggestion that you not use the joiner like a trim saw (for shadow joints, etc.), which is one of the recommended uses for all the competing machines.

Illus. 23-4. Note the convenient switch for right-handers.

Illus. 23-5. This view of the face shows the comfortable handle.

Illus. 23-6. The three-position depth-of-cut scale may be all you'll ever need.

A very well designed flap face (Illus. 23-7) gives easy, true vertical adjustment, and correctly cuts mitres from the outside (Illus. 23-8 and 23-9). The machine has accurate scales on the front (Illus. 23-10) and good centerlines on the front, sides, and bottom. Unfortunately, there are many loose pieces when the flap-face plate is removed (Illus. 23-11). Removing a pair of allen screws from the fixed faceplate reveals the machine's inside mechanisms (Illus. 23-12–23-14).

The machine comes with a 17-millimetre spindle wrench, but I had to use my own $^{15}/_{16}$-inch wrench to remove the blade. The blade

Illus. 23-7. A close-up of the flap face.

Illus. 23-8 and 23-9.
The Bosch fence is terrific
for square cuts and for cutting 45-degree mitres from
the outside.

Illus. 23-9.

Illus. 23-10. A top view
of the front of the unit
shows the convenient lay-
out scales.

Illus. 23-11 (above left). Removing the flap unit is the first step in getting the machine running. **Illus. 23-12 (above right).** Remove the straight face with an allen key.

Illus. 23-13. When these parts are removed . . .

Illus. 23-14. . . . This is what you'll see.

(Illus. 23-15) has four teeth, in contrast to the six found on most machines, and the 12 offered on some sophisticated machines.

The machine was recorded at 92 dB at arm's length, which makes it just about average in the noise department. At 6 pounds, it is of average weight.

According to the manufacturer, this tool has been put through serious safety and function tests, and the plastic casting failure rate has been surprisingly low. If the casting breaks, you may get some resistance from the distributor, but Bosch will replace the tool. The unit is fully functional with the possible exception that to get a completely square setup on the front fence, you have to use setup blocks. The bottom line is that this is not a great product, but it isn't a bad one either.

Illus. 23-15. The Bosch blade (foreground) compared to an older Elu blade and the current Makita blade.

24
Makita 3901 Biscuit Joiner

At the time of this writing, the Makita 3901 biscuit joiner is new to the United States market. Testing this joiner has convinced me that this is a great mid-priced machine.

The Makita 3901 biscuit joiner is a high-quality tool (Illus. 24-1 and 24-2). The rubber cord is 100 inches long. The 5.6-amp, 590-watt motor runs the blade at 10,000 RPM. A dust bag is standard (Illus. 24-3), but the swivelling dust chute also fits the standard Makita dust hose that connects my random orbit sander to my bench vac, so that's how I'd run the machine in my shop. The joiner runs at 92 dB, which makes it among the quietest joiners available. It weighs only 6.2 pounds.

Illus. 24-1. The Makita 3901 joiner in its case.

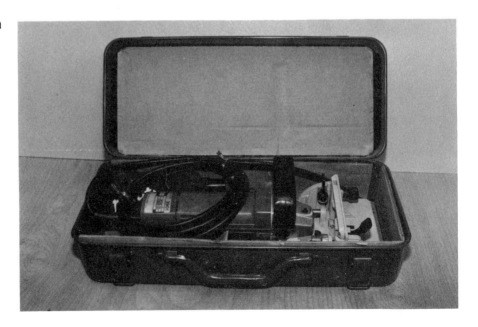

Illus. 24-2. The underside of the joiner shows the carefully polished surface.

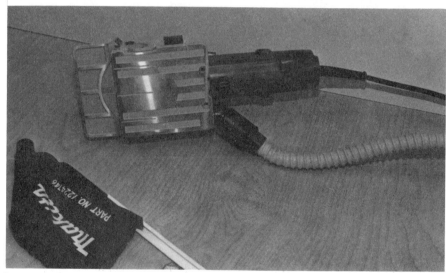

Illus. 24-3. The Makita joiner with the accessory dust hose and the standard dust bag. The hose is an option I can really recommend.

The machine's castings are beautifully machined, equal to those on any other biscuit joiner, and superior to most. This is important, because there is essentially no room for lateral error in biscuit joining. If the cutter is running off square, the error is doubled. As the mating slots are aligned, they *must* be parallel.

Unlike most competing machines, the Makita 3901 joiner provides easy access to the blade. To release the catch, you only have to make two counterclockwise revolutions on the holder bolt. This done, the bottom panel pivots from the front to reveal the blade (Illus. 24-4). Thus, access to the blade is easier on this joiner than on

Illus. 24-4. The bottom of this Makita joiner is open, and a look at its underside reveals a tool that is a marvel of simplicity.

any other, and far easier than most others. After you've gained access to the blade, a shaft lock helps provide easy blade changes.

The large grip face (Illus. 24-5), many times larger than that on the Lamello Top-Ten, can be snapped in and out easily for operations where you want the tool to slide, as when slotting for splines rather than biscuits or when cutting shadow joints along the edges of European-style panelled ceilings. What's more, one of the three optional saw blades makes cutting non-biscuit joints far easier. The maximum depth of cut is ¾ inch with the biscuit-joining blade,

Illus. 24-5. The easily removable non-skid pad. Every manufacturer's skid reducer should be this good — and this easy to use!

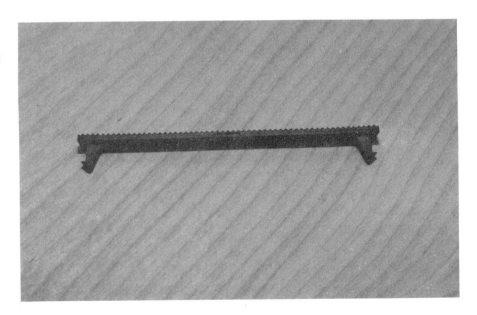

but 1 inch with the optional blades. Other joiner manufacturers don't make this option readily available.

Six cutting depths can be preset by rotating the depth-of-cut adjustment knob; most mid-priced joiners offer only settings for the #0, #10, and #20 biscuits. A large, comfortable tool grip eliminates the need for left-handers like myself to have to turn the European-style D-handle around, although if I keep the tool for use in my shop, I'm likely to modify it with the new Lamello accessory handle.

The front fence adjusts easily from 0 degrees to 90 degrees

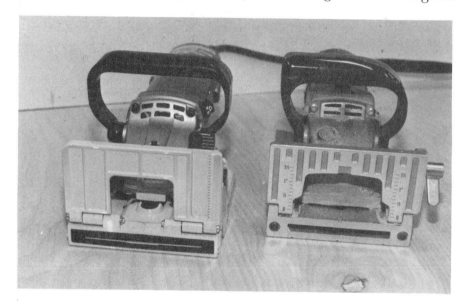

Illus. 24-6. Comparing the fronts of the Makita and Lamello Top-Ten joiners.

Illus. 24-7. Comparing the sides of the Makita and Lamello Top-Ten joiners.

(Illus. 24-6 and 24-7). Most mid-priced joiners require some sort of shimming to achieve angles of other than 0 degrees or 90 degrees. This flap face will save woodworkers a great deal of time.

The Makita joiner's lock-downs (position tighteners) are on the inside of the mechanism rather than on the outside. Thus, on the Makita, as on no other joiner, the center mark for the blade is in fact on the center of the tool. For example, the center mark on the Makita joiner is approximately 2½ inches from the left *and* right. On the Lamello Top-Ten, it is 2⁷⁄₁₆ inches from the right and 3¼ inches from the left. Every other joiner's lock-downs have a potential for interfering with the work.

Also, the Makita joiner's lock-down is inside the accessory fence. The flush sides permit work in very tight spots. On the Lamello fence, one must align a pair of measurements with a pair of indicators to ensure it is square. The Makita's fence runs on a very positive, square rack-and-pinion mechanism that permits precise depth settings with an excellent depth-of-cut scale. After adjusting the mechanism very slightly for square after sliding it onto the machine, it will remain square through many readjustments.

While the angle-adjust scale on the Lamello Top-Ten offers a finer gradation of the numbers, the Makita joiner has positive stop detents at 0 degrees, 45 degrees, and 90 degrees. On the sides of

Illus. 24-8. A close-up of the working portion of the Makita joiner.

the machine (Illus. 24-8), there is a centerline cast for the blade. I had to scribe the sides of my Lamello Top-Ten with a knife to make a centerline. Like the Lamello Top-Ten, the Makita joiner is set up for free-flap cutting in ¾-inch-thick stock; a spacer for cutting in ½-inch-thick stock can be easily added in any shop.

In summary, the Makita 3901 joiner is the first non-Lamello machine that I'm confident I could live with as my only biscuit joiner. I intend to use this machine instead of my Lamello Top-Ten for all my projects over the next several months. This is a real vote of confidence.

25
Commercial Accessories

Ever anxious to make a good product better and to profit from after-market sales, the various joiner manufacturers have introduced a variety of accessories. Lamello is the major manufacturer of accessories for plate joining. It even sells an entire joining system. Most of the accessories discussed here are, in fact, components of the Lamello system. Some of these accessories are genuine innovations, and others appear to be devices designed to profit from the typical (American?) craftsperson's desire to acquire gadgets. Remember, all the accessories discussed here, with the possible exception of the Nova and the Mini-Spot, will more or less work as well with a non-Lamello plate joiner. Following is a survey of the accessory market that will hopefully separate those useful devices from the useless ones.

Gluers

The Lamello Minicol gluer, shown in Illus. 25-1, is the handiest accessory for plate joining. Though it is expensive, it is extremely useful (Illus. 25-2–25-5). It is made of plastic and has a wooden base. You can store the glue bottle upside down so that the glue is always near the tip of the bottle and is ready to be used immediately all the time. The metal tip releases the glue through a pair of channels on opposing sides, thus delivering the glue to the sides of the cut slots. This is a definite advantage and will save a great deal of glue at assembly time. Your next bottle of glue will probably last twice as long.

Joining the popular Minicol gluer is the Lamello Dosicol metered automatic glue bottle (Illus. 25-1). Every biscuit joiner user should seriously consider using this valuable accessory. The glue and time saved using this gluer will more than compensate for its cost.

Illus. 25-1. The Lamello Minicol glue bottle flanked by a pair of Lamello Dosicol glue bottles.

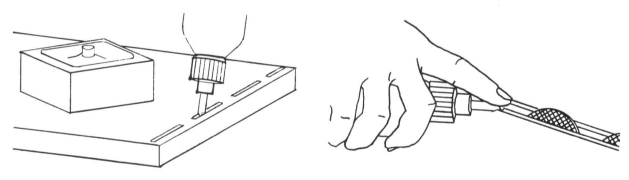

Illus. 25-2–25-5. The Lamello glue bottle is useful for gluing biscuit slots (above left), the slotted surfaces themselves (above right), slots for unusual biscuit configurations (below left), and for internal gluing (below right). (Courtesy of Colonial Saw)

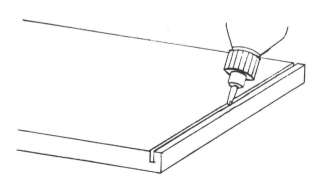

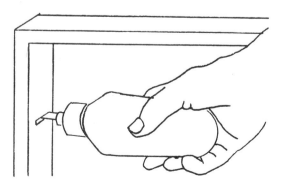

The head on a Wolfcraft glue bottle fits a standard glue bottle (Illus. 25-6). The biscuit-shaped head spreads the glue if you spread it in the slot. The bottle is made of nonporous polypropylene and can be very easily cleaned. While the Dosicol and Wolfcraft glue bottles are reasonable choices, it seems to me that bottles such as the Lamello Minicol are the best for most users.

Green Dolphin Co. sells four gluing aids that are as good as but *markedly* less expensive than similar products. Here we'll consider only the company's biscuit spreader (Illus. 25-7). The device screws onto your regular glue bottle. The plastic glue inserter looks a great deal like the metal spreader marketed by Lamello, but it's much less expensive. This version lacks the wet base which supports the Lamello version upside down when it's not in use, but it comes with a very serviceable cap. Because it does not have a wet base, there will be some drying of glue. As long as all you're using is PVA glues (white or yellow), the dried glue can be soaked off in

Illus. 25-6. The WolfCraft Gluer comes with a bottle, but its tip will attach to standard-size glue bottles.

Illus. 25-7. The tip of the Green Dolphin gluer. Users must supply their own bottles.

water. This spreader has to be soaked more often than others. Perhaps the best approach to using this spreader is to buy two of them and continually soak one.

The Green Dolphin gluing kits are designed for use with PVA glues. Other adhesives, such as resorcinol, urea-formaldehyde, and epoxies, can be used, though cleanup will be considerably more difficult. Limited pot life and the great viscosity of these adhesives may limit their usefulness with the Green Dolphin gluing kit. The plastic components are *not* affected by solvents such as lacquer thinner or acetone. If I were using a glue other than PVA (although I can't imagine why I would) with my biscuit joinery, I might be inclined to use one of these inexpensive Green Dolphin spreaders as a "throw-away."

Lamello has introduced its inexpensive Servicol models (Illus. 25-8 and 25-9) to compete with these economy glue bottles. The tips are plastic rather than metal (like the tips on the Minicol bottle) and they lack the wood block base of the more expensive model. If needed, a wood block base can be made quite quickly. I drilled a ½-inch hole through the top of a block of wood, and then counter-bored the hole $^{17}\!/_{32}$ inch about halfway through. It wouldn't be hard to add a hole at the bottom that's $2\frac{3}{8}$ inches in diameter, and ¼ inch deep, to completely enclose the base. This done, the Servicol serves as nicely as any gluer on the market.

 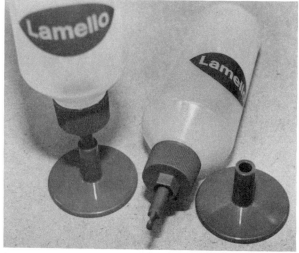

Illus. 25-8 (above left). A view of the larger Servicol and the Green Dolphin gluer heads. **Illus. 25-9 (above right).** The Lamello Servicol in its base and free of its base.

Dust-Collection Systems

Lamello, Virutex, and Bosch each have vacuum hoses on the market for collecting the dust thrown by their joiners; while I haven't figured out the reason why these dust-collection systems are so expensive, it doesn't take long to figure out their usefulness. With a dust-collection system in place, the joiner runs so cleanly that you can run it in the living room, if necessary. These dust pick-up units take a little time to install, though, so after the installation, most people "plug" the power cord into the receptacle and the dust-hose attachment into the vacuum cleaner. Lamello's dust-collection system (Illus. 25-10), at 134 inches, is almost a yard longer than the Virutex counterpart, and its hose is smoother on the inside. The best way to run the unit with the dust pickup accessory is to attach the hose to the power cord with narrow pieces of duct tape, and then operate the tool with the cord and the vacuum hose both thrown over your shoulder. The dust pickup kit is necessary, especially if you are left-handed (Illus. 25-11). The availability of this accessory should be a prime consideration when choosing a joiner, even if you elect not to purchase the pickup right away.

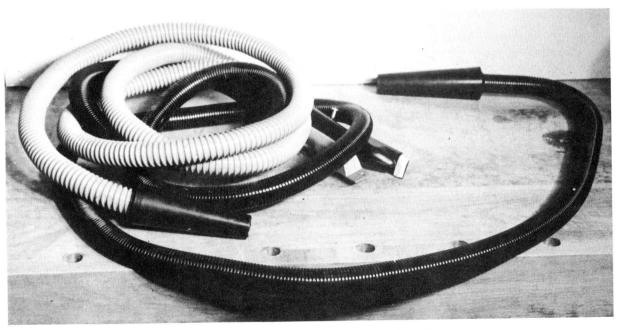

Illus. 25-10. The Lamello dust-collection kit, the darker of the pair shown here, is nearly a yard longer than the Virutex kit shown with it.

Illus. 25-11. This left-handed operator really wishes there were a dust collector attached to the joiner he is using.

Lamello Hinge-Mounting System

Lamello's hinge-mounting system has to be one of the best solutions I've encountered to the problem of hinge mortising. Lamello Paumelle hinges comes in three types: bright nickel, black, and solid brass. Each hinge will hold 22 pounds, so it may be necessary to use more than a single pair in some operations. The hinges are sold as "left" and "right," so they can be used in combinations for non-removable doors, or separately for doors that can be lifted out of position (Illus. 25-12 and 25-13).

Illus. 25-12. Lamello hinges and plates are now available in small quantities for occasional users.

Illus. 25-13. Lamello Paumelle hinges are strong, attractive, and easy to mount. The pair shown here is for both left- and right-hand mounting. You can use mixed hinged types for doors that are to be attached in place. Since each pair of hinges can hold about 20 pounds, more than a single pair may be required for large doors.

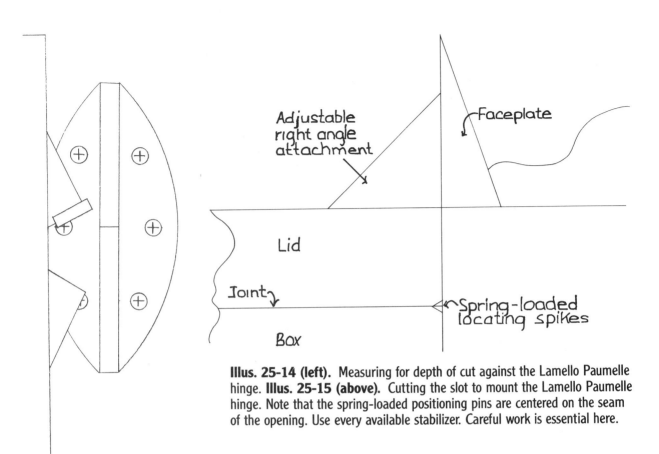

Adjustable right angle attachment

Faceplate

Lid

Joint

Box

Spring-loaded locating spikes

Illus. 25-14 (left). Measuring for depth of cut against the Lamello Paumelle hinge. **Illus. 25-15 (above).** Cutting the slot to mount the Lamello Paumelle hinge. Note that the spring-loaded positioning pins are centered on the seam of the opening. Use every available stabilizer. Careful work is essential here.

Illus. 25-16. Lamello Paumelle hinges can be used in various applications. A: They can be used on folding partitions and doors. Lamello hinges offer easy removal of doors for cleaning and moving. B: They can be used on drop leaves and doors. Rotate one hinge for fast, permanent installation. C: The hinges are perfect for box lids and full-overlay cabinets. D: Lamello hinges can be used on flush cabinet doors for European styling.

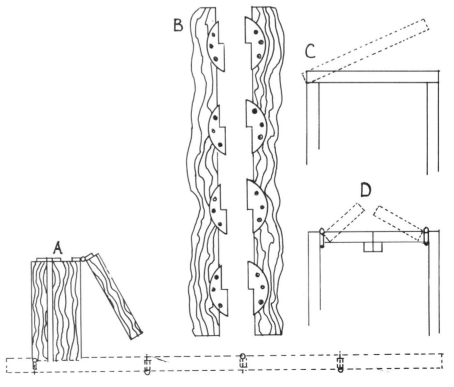

These high-fashion hinges, regarded by some as the "hallmark of contemporary furniture," can be quickly installed. After you have sawn your box open and smoothed and squared the opening, clamp the door to the body. Mark out hinge locations with a pair of simple pencil scribes. Position the plate joiner so that it is centered exactly on the seam. Cut kerfs the size of number 20 biscuits for each hinge. Unclamp and separate the door from the carcass. Set the hinges loosely in place. Punch through the screw holes with an awl (Illus. 25-17). Screw the hinges in place.

Illus. 25-17. The Lamello awl is made specifically to install Lamello Paumelle hinges.

Lamello's awl is surely handier than the hammerlike version that I have used in the past for many years. Despite its high price, a regular user of Lamello Paumelle hinges may find this awl to be superior to other available awls or to the drill-centering bits (sold sometimes as Vix-Bits) (Illus. 25-18).

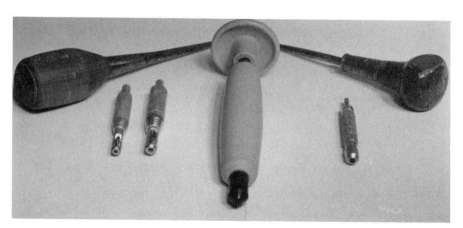

Illus. 25-18. The Lamello awl with a Stanley center-ing awl, a pair of standard scratch awls, and a pair of Vix-Bits.

Lamello Lamex Knockdown Fittings

Lamello recommends the Lamello Lamex knockdown fittings for panel, leaf assemblies, and shelves. The plastic inserts come in white or brown, as shown in Illus. 25-19. The wooden biscuits, size 20 only, are fibre-reinforced (Illus. 25-20). An installation kit, shown in Illus. 25-21, makes things easier by allowing rapid and accurate cutting of the T slot for the connecting part. The kit is not a necessity, but I would not care to install these fittings without it. It makes their installation accurate and quick; while installing Lamex

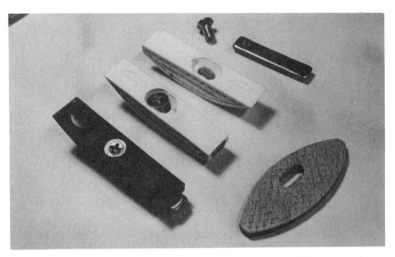

Illus. 25-19. The Lamello Lamex knockdown fittings. This system includes brown and white plastic inserts with adjustable metal clamps (shown disassembled at top), and fibre-reinforced size-20 biscuits.

Illus. 25-20. This Lamex biscuit has been severed with a knife, and only after great effort, to reveal the fibres.

Illus. 25-21. The Lamello Lamex installation kit offers a complete method for joining units that must be frequently disassembled.

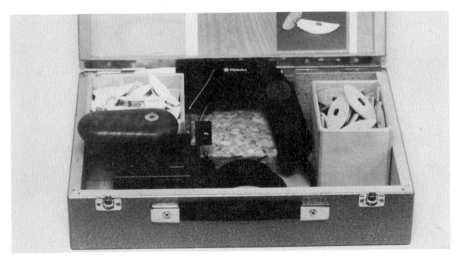

fittings freehand is possible, it will take too much time and will not be accurate for most jobs.

To install the Lamex system, align the pieces to be joined as in a regular biscuit-joined operation; cut the mating slots, and glue the special wooden biscuits in place, as shown in Illus. 25-22. Place the Lamex cutter gauge, shown in Illus. 25-23, in a slot on the other side, and make three or four plunge cuts, all the way through the "swing" of the gauge (Illus. 25-24). Set the Lamex connectors into these milled cuts, and glue them into place with the hot-glue gun, as

Illus. 25-22. Here are the "biscuit" ends of the Lamex knockdown clamping system.

Illus. 25-23. A close-up of the Lamex cutter gauge that shows its relationship to the biscuit slot, to which it is cutting a wide perpendicular slot.

Illus. 25-24. The Lamex gauge at work.

Illus. 25-25. Gluing the Lamex connectors in place with a hot-glue gun.

shown in Illus. 25-25. (I imagine that in this case a neat epoxy job could be done instead.) After all the adhesives have set, insert the biscuits into their mating holes and tighten the screws (Illus. 25-26). The result is a tight, removable (and thus portable) joint, a joint whose tightness can be adjusted. This may well be the finest system that I have encountered for making knockdown furniture.

As I have said of too many of these accessories, Lamex fittings are expensive. So is the installation kit, which consists of a cutting gauge, a glue gun, a case, and some samples.

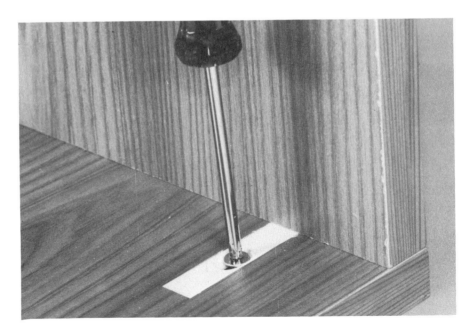

Illus. 25-26. Here a clamp is being tightened into place. The clamps work equally well both horizontally and vertically.

Lamello Spanner Set

The Lamello spanner set can be bought in a variety of ways. You can buy the entire set, which consists of two clamps that have 8 metres of belting each, two tension hooks, and four 24-inch aluminum profile corner protectors. If all you want is the spanner itself, you can buy one pair of clamps that have 5 metres of belting. Clamps can also be bought without belting, and the nylon belting can be bought separately. So can the tension hooks (per pair), 24-inch profile corner protectors (per set of four), the 5-inch profile corner protectors (per set of four), and the 16¼-inch profile corner protectors (Illus. 25-27). As expensive as it is, the Lamello spanner set is one of the most useful clamping systems available on the market, and it is a great enhancement to any joining system.

The advantage of the Lamello spanner set is that a woodworker can quickly glue up carcasses that might otherwise be impossible to glue up when he is working alone. It also helps ensure that the joints are drawn tight. For carcass work, the Lamello spanner set is much handier than using bar or pipe clamps, and it may leave the carcass light enough to be moved if necessary. To use it in carcass construction, simply set the "bottom" joint in the extrusion with sufficient webbing to span the unit hanging out proportionally. Assemble the carcass. Set the remaining pair of extrusions on the "top" joints, and "set" the clamp tightly.

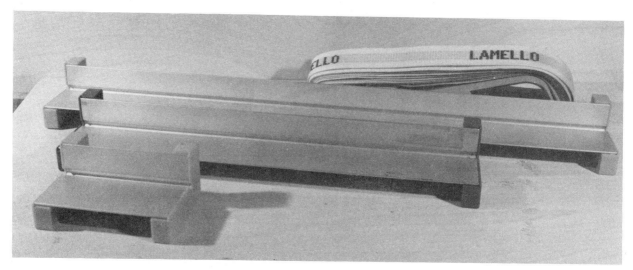

Illus. 25-27. The Lamello spanner set can now be used with three different sizes of corners.

After you have made the final adjustments for square, tighten the clamps (Illus. 25-28 and 25-29).

At first, the spanner set seems less handy for flat-clamping. However, when a standard pipe or bar clamp is tightened, you can move the work slightly by rotating it clockwise. The spanner set does a better job of maintaining flat, true work, particularly in thicker stock.

One drawback of using the spanner set is that you will have to be extremely careful when using glue. The webbing of the Lamello spanner kit won't last long with glue spilled all over it. If you are using the spanner with biscuit-joined assemblies, there should be little if any seepage.

The Lamello spanner set is a clamping system that may replace eight or more pipe clamps in carcass construction and is immeasurably quicker than other clamping systems. If time means money in your shop, as it does in mine, and if you expect to always get first-class results, the Lamello spanner set may have a place in your shop. If, however, the price remains an obstacle, consider having your woodworker's guild or club buy a set for the occasional use of all the members.

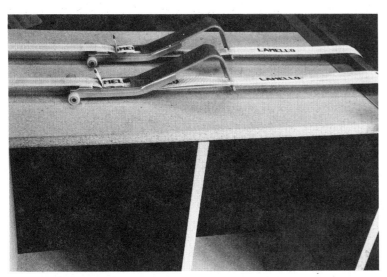 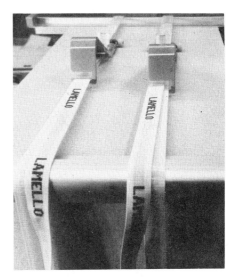

Illus. 25-28 (above left). The Lamello spanner at work. **Illus. 25-29 (above right).** The Lamello spanner shown over the 24-inch corner protectors.

Lamello Mini-Spot Patching Kit

The Lamello Mini-Spot, shown in Illus. 25-30, is a tool that has very little value in the typical American cabinet shop. I am so accustomed to treating in a different way the problem that the Lamello Mini-Spot addresses that I found this attachment to be expensive far beyond its value to me. Basically, the Mini-Spot consists of a spear-point saw blade and a special faceplate for the Lamello Junior joiner. After the plate joiner has been converted, simply run it over pitch pockets or similar defects, and then glue in patches that Lamello sells separately in various wood species (Illus. 25-31). After the glue has set, pare the patch flush to the surface.

This procedure is as involving as the one I use to solve the same problem. I cut out my stock in four- to six-inch widths for gluing, using the defects as markings for cutting lines. The Mini-Spot would make it possible to use wider boards if you had a project where wider boards would be genuinely desirable, and if you could keep those wide boards from warping.

Part of my objection to the tool is that one must take a few minutes to set up the machine for the Mini-Spot application, an important consideration in shops where the price of labor is almost always higher than the price of materials. But even this is secondary to the visibility of the patch, which at best looks no better to me than a shop-cut circular plug.

Illus. 25-30. The Lamello Mini-Spot patching kit attached in place on a joiner.

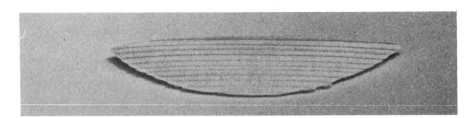

Illus. 25-31. A Mini-Spot patch made of pine. These patches are also available in maple, ash, cherry, beech, spruce, and other species.

Lamello Nova Edge Trimmer

The Lamello Nova edge trimmer shown in Illus. 25-32 and 25-33 is an attachment that is probably of most use to kitchen installers. You can attach it to any Lamello machine quickly with a pair of heavy screws; an adjusting screw permits the blade to contact the cabinet flush and makes it possible to trim a face frame flush with the edge of the cabinet. However, it doesn't seem to be sufficiently superior or quicker than trimming with a flush-sided dovetail saw and a strip of sandpaper, as I have always done in the past. And the flush-cutting dovetail saw is just a fraction of the price of the Nova. If I were a professional kitchen installer, I might want a Nova permanently installed on a Junior; this way, the savings in time would eventually pay for the tool.

The Bosch and Elu joiner/groovers seem to be easily better than the Nova for performing this operation. The Bosch machine will do edge trimming to a depth of $\frac{7}{8}$ inch with the biscuit-slotting blade or with a very fine 22-tooth (2.2-mm) blade. The combina-

Illus. 25-32. A joiner with the Nova attachment in place.

Illus. 25-33. The Lamello Nova edge trimmer can be quickly and easily fitted to your Lamello joiner for trimming protruding edges with great precision.

tion of Bosch's small size, handy rip fence, generally well-designed body, and fine blades make this machine much handier than the Lamello Nova or a standard portable circular saw for this sort of edge trimming. The Elu's lateral blade adjustment permits it to complete this task with amazing accuracy.

Lamello Inserta Pneumatic Biscuit Installer

If you are going to use your joiner in a production shop, you may be interested in the new Lamello Inserta, shown in Illus. 25-34–25-36.

Illus. 25-34. The Lamello Inserta pneumatic biscuit installer.

Illus. 25-35. This front view of the Lamello Inserta shows the prongs that guarantee dead-center insertion every time.

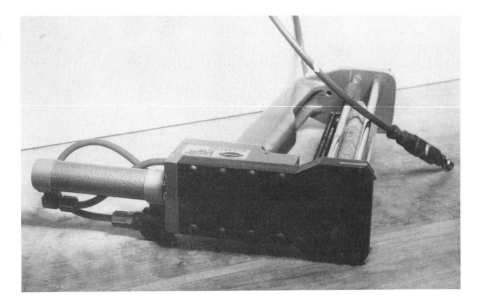

Illus. 25-36. A close-up of the working end of the Lamello Inserta.

This low-maintenance pneumatic machine holds 50 biscuits, and the biscuits can be hand-loaded or purchased in a special Inserta pack for quick loading. An ingenious quick-release mechanism for loading permits the spring tension to be held off the plates while freeing the locator arm for loading the biscuits. Colonial Saw calls the market for this tool "somewhat limited," and its high list price is undoubtedly a contributing factor to that limited marketplace.

Lamello Universal Handle

Illus. 25-37 compares the Lamello Universal Handle to the D-handle that is standard on biscuit joiners. This inexpensive accessory fits most of the currently available joiners (Illus. 25-38 and 25-39). This handle is far superior to the D-handle. I do have one reservation concerning this handle: Old-time woodworkers are used to operating the tool by its motor body rather than by its D-handle, and are sure to prefer *that* handle to this new one.

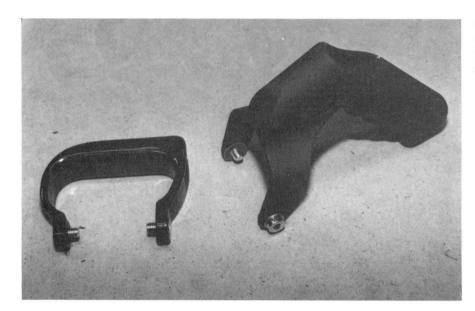

Illus. 25-37. The ergonomic Lamello Universal handle (right) compared to the standard D-handle.

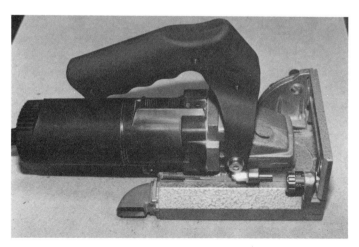

Illus. 25-38. The Lamello Universal handle mounted on the Lamello Top-Ten.

Illus. 25-39. The hand is positioned on the Lamello handle to show its basic comfort and convenience.

Lamello Stationary Attachment

Lamello has just released an attachment for mounting Junior joiners to stationary columns; it even has its own ratchet version of this attachment (Illus. 25-40 and 25-41). Lamello recommends these attachments, especially for use with the Lamello Mini-Spot attachment, but they might also be useful for joining small pieces.

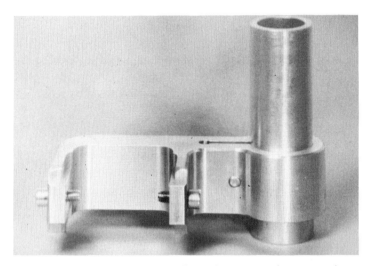

Illus. 25-40 (above). The Lamello stationary attachment can be used for mounting to any stationary column. **Illus. 25-41 (right.)** The Lamello stationary attachment mounted to a drill press apparatus.

Lamello Assista Positioning Jig

The Lamello Assista is a positioning jig that can be used with all Lamello biscuit joiners (Illus. 25-42). It provides fast, easy setup for uniform, repeatable joint spacings on faces, edges, and mitres when you adjust it to 90, 45, and 0 degrees. Inlaid rubber and completely adjustable clamps hold the Assista precisely in place (Illus. 25-43). A detent gives smooth, easy positioning of the unit (Illus. 25-44). An index mark permits instant workpiece positioning (Illus. 25-45 and 25-46). Using this indexing system provides faster, more accurate biscuit joinery than any strictly "hand" method that I know. If you need quick, accurate work, this accessory may be just what is needed (Illus. 25-47 and 25-48).

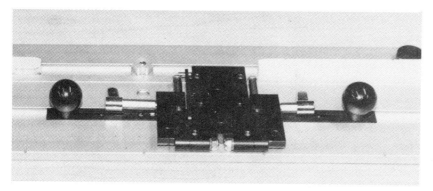

Illus. 25-42 (above). Top view of the working portion of the Assista jig.
Illus. 25-43 (right). This view of the Assista's underside shows a pair of rubber tracks (which hold the base in place almost well enough to require no clamping) and one of a pair of sliding clamps, which can be positioned anywhere under the jig.

Illus. 25-44 (above left). This close-up of the Assista jig shows the detents, which ensure accurate angles. **Illus. 25-45 and 25-46 (center and right).** These two photos show how the adjustable detents help to position the work uniformly for repeated work.

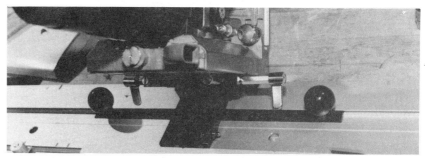

Illus. 25-47 (left). To fasten the Lamello joiner to the Assista, you have to tighten a pair of allen screws through the jig into the bottom of the machine. The extra-long allen wrench shown on the left here is not standard equipment with the jig. **Illus. 25-48 (above).** Here the Lamello Top-Ten is mounted in the Assista, ready to make a 45-degree mitred slot.

Illus. 25-49 contains the operating instructions Lamello supplies with this tool.

Mounting the machine

1. Set pushing unit vertical
2. Lower guides of pushing unit
3. Remove tips with springs (anti-slip pads) on the machine
4. Screw machine secure to pushing unit
5. Set machine to desired angle 90°, 45° or 0° and engage support

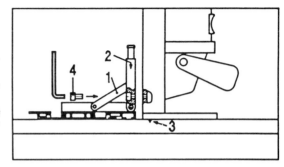

Cutting-in vertical (90°)

1. Position guide template on workpiece and fix it
2. Release both clamp levers on pushing unit and lower the machine onto the workpiece
3. Adjust distance template
4. Position machine in index notch

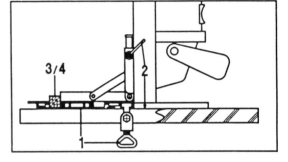

Cutting-in to mitre (45°)

1. Fix guide template on flat surface
2. Align workpiece with guide template (for thin material: use underlay)
3. Release both clamp levers on pushing unit and push the machine to the workpiece
4. Adjust distance template
5. Position machine in index notch

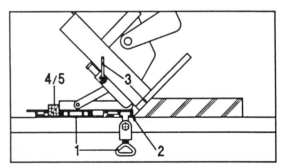

Cutting-in horizontal (0°)

1. Fix guide template on flat surface
2. Release both clamp levers on pushing unit and align machine flush with guide template
3. Use plate 22 mm thick as supporting surface; place workpiece on it and align with guide template
4. Adjust distance template
5. Position machine in index notch

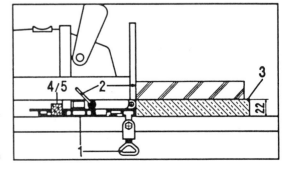

Illus. 25-49. Instructions for using the Lamello Assista.

Face-Framing Accessories

Many of the professional woodworkers I encounter have the same negative comment about biscuit joinery. "It's a great tool," they tell me, "but it's absolutely useless when it comes to making face frames, and that's a big part of my job." Until lately, this was all too true. Several manufacturers, including CFW Engineering, Woodhaven, and even Lamello, have introduced tools for joining face frames and other small joints more quickly.

Woodhaven is a direct-marketing company whose founder, Bradd Witt, has introduced many novel tools to woodworkers. His Biscuit Miter Jig is perhaps the least-expensive method of biscuiting narrow material (Illus. 25-50). This inexpensive jig makes routing slots in end grain both safer and easier than other methods. The jig is designed to be used on an existing router table with a fence and one stop. Use the jig by sliding the entire jig and the related workpiece along the stop and into the bit and making a plunge cut, which is what Woodhaven biscuits require. Witt notes

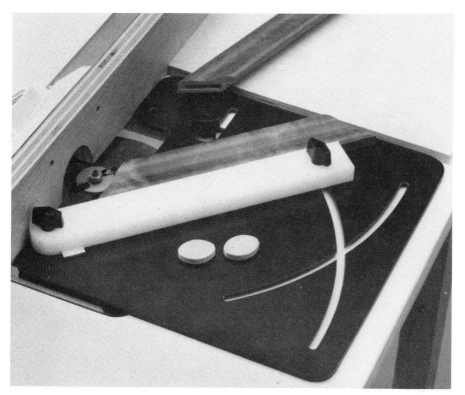

Illus. 25-50. The Woodhaven biscuit mitre jig provides a safer and easier method of routing biscuit slots in mitred end cuts. It will cut any mitred end grain from 90 to 45 degrees. When 90-degree cuts are made, the stock can be a maximum width of 8 inches. When 45-degree cuts are made, the stock can be a maximum width of 3 inches.

that if you insist on using regular biscuits and a standard slotting cutter, you will need to set up an additional stop on your table to make an elongated slot. The jig will handle any mitred end grain from 90 to 45 degrees. Stock width is limited to a minimum 8 inches wide at 90 degrees and 3 inches wide at 45 degrees (Illus. 25-51– 25-53). By making a simple auxiliary fence to attach to the jig's regular fence, you can cut bevels and compound mitres. The jig is accompanied by a very clear instruction manual.

Illus. 25-51. Woodhaven biscuits in place in very narrow stock.

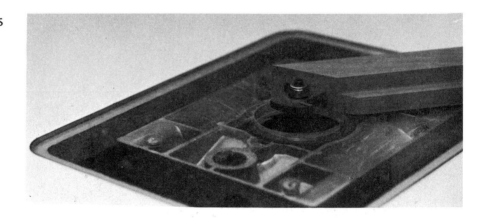

Illus. 25-52. Cutting slots with a Woodhaven slotting cutter on a Woodhaven router table.

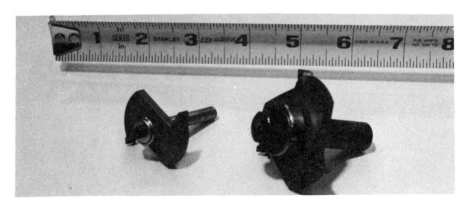

Illus. 25-53. Woodhaven slotting cutter (left) and the "standard" slotting cutter from my shop.

The Woodhaven jig is best used with one (or both!) of their "Biscuits & Bits" kits (Illus. 25-54 and 25-55). I'm pleased to note that the Biscuit Miter Jig eliminates the reservations I expressed about Woodhaven's Biscuits & Bits kit in this book's previous edition. While it is possible to use the kits freehand, it's easy to smash a knuckle doing this. The new chip-limitation design on the slotting bit will help eliminate any possibility of kickback, but the jig will still be helpful in terms of both accuracy and safety.

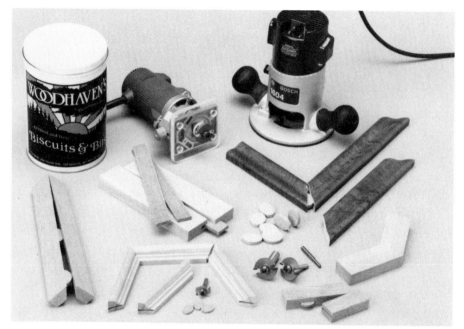

Illus. 25-54. Woodhaven's Biscuits & Bits kit.

Illus. 25-55. Woodhaven's new Itty Bitty Biscuits & Bits kit may provide the best method of all for joining very narrow or thin stock.

The biscuits in the Biscuits & Bits kit are designed to fit *exactly* into the plunge cut made with the slotting bit. The bearing on the bit controls the depth of cut; a straight cutter is provided for plunging into the faces of workpieces where a slotting-style bit will not work, such as uprights of bookshelves; this is usually less than 10 percent of your joinery. The router can be used in "portable" mode for large pieces. The bit's small diameter and narrow kerf provide terrific control and little chance of pulling or grabbing. The Woodhaven biscuits are made of a grainless compressed wood-fibre composition board, sanded to close tolerance for accurate fit. These biscuits are cut just slightly small so you have some lateral adjustment in the joint, as you would with a regular biscuit.

Woodhaven's original biscuit has a $1\frac{1}{2}$-inch diameter and makes a cut $\frac{1}{2}$ inch deep by $1\frac{3}{8}$ inches long and $\frac{15}{64}$ inch wide. It is used with a bit that has a $\frac{1}{2}$-inch-diameter bearing. It will work in stock that is at least $1\frac{1}{2}$ inches wide for 90-degree butt joints, and in stock at least $1\frac{3}{16}$ inches wide for 45-degree mitre joints. The stock should have a minimum thickness of $\frac{1}{2}$ inch. In thicker stock, you can stack the biscuits. The slotting bit is available with a $\frac{1}{4}$- or $\frac{1}{2}$-inch shank, but the straight bit is available only with a $\frac{1}{4}$-inch shank.

Woodhaven's new Itty Bitty Biscuits & Bits kit is ideal for picture framing or similar joinery in narrow or thin stock. This smaller-size bit is 1 inch in diameter with a $\frac{3}{8}$-inch bearing and makes a cut $\frac{5}{16}$ inch deep, $\frac{15}{16}$ inch long, and $\frac{1}{8}$ inch wide. It will work in minimum 1-inch-wide stock for 90-degree butt joints, and minimum $\frac{3}{4}$-inch-wide stock for 45-degree mitres. Otherwise, the stock should be a minimum of $\frac{1}{4}$ inch thick. If you require a straight bit, any $\frac{1}{8}$-inch bit will work.

In many ways, these Woodhaven kits help to resolve the problem of face-frame joining with a biscuit joiner. Nevertheless, if you have to move many face frames through your shop in a limited amount of time, there are some other items worth considering. CFW Engineering has introduced a complete line of benchtop biscuit joiners with which you do not have to clamp the workpieces. The three CFW joiners are more sophisticated, and much more expensive, than other biscuit joiners. Of most interest to woodworkers is probably the model 100 joiner (Illus. 25-56–25-58). This is the original machine designed for use with model C biscuits. These biscuits are 4 millimetres thick, 24 millimetres wide, and 33 millimetres long. A box of 1,000 model C biscuits contains four bags

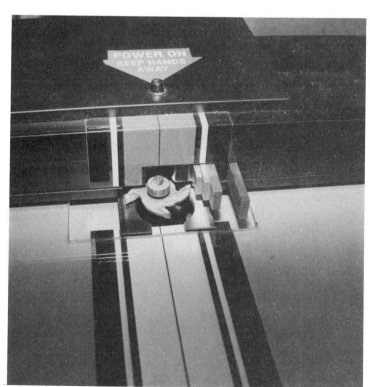

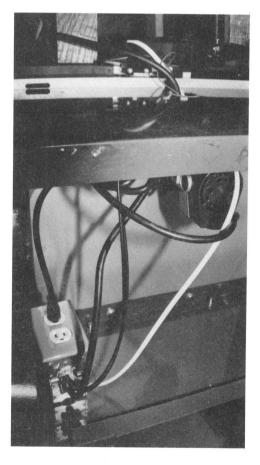

Illus. 25-57 (above left). The CFW model 100 joiner with its cutterhead and stops exposed. Note the switch plates under the cutterhead and stop. **Illus. 25-58 (right).** The CFW model 100 joiner has an elaborate switching system.

of 250. Model C biscuits are the same thickness as regular joining biscuits but they are the width of a #20 biscuit and are shorter than the Lamello H9 biscuits, which require a special cutter in a standard joiner (Illus. 25-59 and 25-60).

The model 100 joiner has an "auto-start/no-start" safety system: The machine goes on when a workpiece is placed against the fence, but the cutter motor will not operate when the carriage is moved rearwards without a workpiece in place. The rotating blade is always covered by the sliding carriage or the workpiece. The machine goes off immediately after you're done cutting. A series of four spring-loaded stops for 1½-, 1¾-, 2-, and 3-inch rails takes all the guesswork out of joining. The warranty covers one year of professional or home use.

The sliding fence helps to keep the blade away from your hands. Nevertheless, if you join small pieces, there is more potential for injury with this type of joiner than with the more standard hand-held models. As with all tools, work carefully. The sliding fence is fitted with return springs that should require very little maintenance. The tool appears to be made of first-class materials. While any router cutter could probably be used, the cutter that

Illus. 25-59. From left to right: A CFW C biscuit, a Lamello H 9 biscuit (which requires a special blade), and size 0, 10, and 20 biscuits.

comes with the model 100 joiner is an extra-heavy-duty model. The fence is scribed at the centerline of the cutting tool, and at the edges of the 1½-, 1¾-, 2-, and 3-inch rails. The sliding fence is grooved for efficient removal of chips, but these materials are removed even more efficiently with a vacuum cleaner attachment. An adjustable workpiece stop is so simple an attachment that woodworkers are likely to borrow its design for use on their table saws' mitre gauges, etc. The tool is accompanied by a clear instruction manual. Using the stops is crucial only with very narrow stock or where very precise joints are required. If I made more than a couple of face frames per year, I'd certainly find room for this tool in my shop.

The CFW model 50 kit converts your router table to a stationary plate joiner (Illus. 25-61). It includes a sliding fence assembly, a 1½-inch cutter, 100 C biscuits, decals, and mounting hardware. This model lacks the spring-loaded stops and the feed-pressure-actuated switch of the most sophisticated model.

The CFW model 80 kit consists of a 23-inch sliding fence carriage equipped with a dust-collection chamber, built-in retractable work stops, an adjustable work stop, the "auto-start/no-start" feature found with the model 100 kit, a cutter, and the instructions, decals, and hardware with which to install the joiner on your router table.

Illus. 25-61. The CFW model 50 joiner sitting on a CFW model 100 joiner.

Illus. 25-62. The CFW model 400 joiner.

High-volume shops might appreciate the CFW model 400, which offers fast setup and operation (Illus. 25-62). Its four cutterheads can slot stiles in a single operation, and it neatly slots rails 1½ inches or larger. This machine costs but a fraction of the cost of imported competing models. The advertising material for this machine also suggests that CFW will custom-make a joiner for your specific requirements.

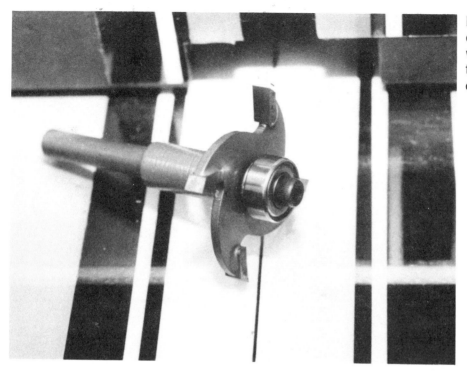

Woodworkers of modest means may prefer to buy just the S-11 cutter from Lamello; this appears to be the same cutter used in the CFW machines (Illus. 25-63). A shop-built jig patterned after one of these professional models might provide all the accuracy you need. Having seen these products, I become even more convinced that biscuit joining is essential to any shop where efficiency and accuracy are important (Illus. 25-64).

Illus. 25-64. A joint cut in 1¾-inch material with a CFW biscuit joiner.

APPENDICES

Glossary

Apron   A downward extension on a piece of furniture that connects the legs.

Base   The underside of the joiner. Good-quality bases have layout lines which help to position cuts.

Bevel   An inclined, angled, or slanted edge.

Biscuit Joiner   A grinder-like device with a spring-loaded faceplate that sets for plunge-cutting slots.

Biscuits   Thin elliptical wooden wafers that are used to join the slots cut by the joiner.

Butt Joint   A joint in which the edge or end of one board is butted against another board.

Carcass   The basic frame of a cabinet.

Dado Joint   A T-shaped joint used to make boxes, cabinets, and shelves.

Depth of Cut   The amount of stock the biscuit joiner blade cuts when controlled by the depth-of-cut adjustment.

D-handle   The front handle on all joiners, which is shaped like the letter D.

Dovetail Joint   A joint in which tapered pins fit into sockets between flared tails.

Dowels   Wooden pegs used in cabinets and bookcases, and to join the parts of a chair or table legs to a rail.

Edge of Stock   The narrower surface of a board which goes with the grain.

Face Frame   The facing structure composed of horizontal and vertical pieces that form the openings for drawers and doors in a furniture piece.

Face Frame Joint   The joint that attaches the hardwood face of furniture to the carcass.

Face of Stock   The wider surface of a board which goes with the grain.

Faceplate   The plate on the front of the joiner. The blade plunges through the faceplate to make the cut for the slot.

Fence   The square or (usually 45°) angled attachment to the joiner's faceplate, which helps determine the position of the joiner's slotting cuts.

Gauge Blocks   Shop-made accessories that help to set up for squarely positioned cuts.

Grain Direction   The orientation of the fibres in the wood.

Hardboard   A sheet material made by compressed wood fibres.

Knockdown Furniture   Furniture that can be easily assembled or disassembled.

Mitre Joint   A joint made by fastening together usually perpendicular cuts with ends made at an angle.

Mortise-and-Tenon Joint   A joint in which a project on one board called a tongue fits into a groove in the other board.

Moulding   A wood surface shape or a narrow strip that is used primarily for decoration.

Offset Joints   Joints that are cut with a shim between the fence and the face of one of the workpieces.

Particleboard   A sheet material made from pressed wood chips or wood particles.

Plywood   A sheet material made by gluing together thin layers of wood.

PVA (Polyvinyl Acetate) Glue   Sometimes called white glue, this is the most common type of woodworking glue. It is commonly used to glue biscuits.

Rabbet Joint   An L-shaped joint that goes along the edge of a piece of stock.

Sheet Stock   Any wood material sold in sheets 4 feet wide and 8 to 12 feet long. Common types of sheet stock include particleboard, plywood, panelling, and hardboard.

Spline   A thin piece of wood that fits into a groove that is cut into both mating surfaces of the joint.

Tongue-and-Groove Joint   A joint in which a projection on one board called a tongue fits into a groove in the other board.

Workpiece   The piece of wood that is being cut or worked.

Biscuit Joiner Features

Maker or Distributor	Model	Retail Price (dollars)	Weight (pounds)	Speed (RPM)	Power Consumption (AMPs)
Black & Decker/ DeWalt/Elu (800-923-8665)	Black & Decker 3382	230	6¼	10,000	6.5
	DeWalt DW 682	222	6¼	10,000	6.5
	Elu 3379	229	6¼	10,000	6.5
Fortune Extendables PrinceCraft/Börg/ Jointmatic	Jointmatic 550	120	7½	10,000	6
Freud	JS-100A	134	7	10,000	5
	JS-102	188	6⅞	10,000	5
Lamello Colonial Saw (800-252-6355)	Top-Ten	538	7¼	10,000	6.4
	Standard-Ten	399	7⅛	10,000	5.8
	Cobra	250	6⅞	10,000	2.1
Makita	Makita 3901		6⅕	10,000	5.6
Porter-Cable (800-487-8665)	555	159	6½	8,000	5
	556	172	6½	8,000	5
PrinceCraft/AMT	4960	165	6⅝	10,000	6
Ryobi (800-525-2579)	JM-100K	209	7¼	9,000	5.3
S-B Power Tools (312-286-7330)	Borch B1650	158	6	11,000	5.8
	Skil HD 1605	123	6	12,000	6
Sears	Craftsman 17501	100	6	10,000	6
	Bis Kit	39	Specifications depend on your router's specifications		
Virutex (800-847-8839)	AB 11C	250	6⅛	10,000	6

Maker or Distributor	Model	Noise Level (Decibels)	Dust-Collection Features	Anti-Slip Features	Angle-Cutting Capabilities	Non-Standard Size Biscuits that can be used
Black & Decker/ DeWalt/Elu (800-923-8665)	Black & Decker 3382	94	bag/vacuum	rubber dots	variable	M
	DeWalt DW 682	94	bag/vacuum	rubber dots	variable	M
	Elu 3379	94	bag/vacuum	rubber dots	variable	M
Fortune Extendables PrinceCraft/Börg/ Jointmatic	Jointmatic 550	96	bag	pins	variable	S/D/M
Freud	JS-100A	92	bag	rubber dots	45°/90°	S/D/M
	JS-102	92	bag	rubber dots	variable	S/D/M
Lamello Colonial Saw (800-252-6355)	Top-Ten	92	vacuum	rubber dots	variable	S/D/M
	Standard-Ten	93	vacuum	rubber dots	45°/90°	S/D/M
	Cobra	94	vacuum	rubber dots	45°/90°	S/D/M
Makita	Makita 3901	92	bag/vacuum	rubber face	variable	S/D/M
Porter-Cable (800-487-8665)	555	93	none	pins	45°/90°	none
	556	93	none	pins	variable	none
PrinceCraft/AMT	4960	94	bag	pins	45°/90°	none
Ryobi (800-525-2579)	JM-100K	96	bag	rubber face	variable	none
S-B Power Tools (312-286-7330)	Borch B1650	94	bag/vacuum	rubber dots	variable	none
	Skil HD 1605	96	bag	none	45°/90°	none
Sears	Craftsman 17501	93	box	rubber face	45°/90°	none
	Bis Kit	Specifications depend on your router's specifications				
Virutex (800-847-8839)	AB 11C	94	vacuum	rubber dots	variable	S/D/M

Index

Acknowledgments

Special thanks to *Popular Woodworking* magazine, and editor David Camp. Additionally, the book could not have been completed without the help of a number of folks from the biscuit joiner manufacturing and distribution business:

Mr. Rick Schmidt and Mr. Dennis Huntsman, Porter-Cable Tools, Jackson, MS

Mr. Jim Brewer, Freud USA, Inc., High Point, NC

Mr. Larry Greenwood, Hafele USA, Inc., Cheyenne, NC

Mr. Leland Nichols, Black & Decker Corp. (DeWalt and Elu), Hunt Valley, MD

Mr. Rick Yorde, Skil Corp., Chicago, IL, and Mr. Joe Karkosch, WolfCraft USA, Itasca, IL

Mr. Jim Larson, Woodworkers Tool Source, Kalamazoo, MI (PrinceCraft)

Mr. Mike Mangan, MKM Communications, Chicago, IL (Sears)

Mr. Perry Martin, Shopsmith, Dayton, OH

Mr. Gene Sliga, Delta International, Pittsburgh, PA

Mr. Jeff Dils, Ryobi America, Inc., Anderson, SC

Mr. Allen Clausen, CFW Engineering, Fallbrook, CA

Mr. Bob Jardinico, Colonial Saw, Inc. (Lamello), Kingston, MA, who provided many of the photos that illustrate the text.

Special thanks to John Anderson and Bill Flemming, who helped with the technical drawings, and to Mike Cea, who turned my manuscript into a book. Like the representatives of the tool companies mentioned above, each deserves more of a thank-you than appears here, for the book reflects the expertise which they have most generously shared with me. Of course, responsibility for any errors and omissions remains my own.